The Order of Freedom

THE ONLY PRINCIPLE THAT CAN SAVE THE WORLD

For Dad

Foreword

The world is upside down. There's chaos everywhere. Many people no longer feel they're taken seriously by politics and the mass media. Trust in politicians, journalists, entrepreneurs and managers is at a low point. The so-called "elite" is morally bankrupt.

More and more people are warming to the libertarian idea that nobody has the right to rule over other people. People from the so-called truth movement are increasingly realizing that it is almost exclusively state institutions that spread sometimes hair-raising lies that mock any common sense. The so-called "refugee crisis" is only the most obvious example here.

It is again the state that, in the case of the crimes of large corporations and banks, does nothing about them or provides them with oligopolies or even the monopoly of money creation. Worse still, those who have done the worst business deals and disregarded customers' wishes the most are saved with taxpayers' money. Many people, however, think that all that's needed is better politicians or a better organisation of power, for example through direct democracy.

In reality, all the social and economic problems we see today are simply the logical result of the fact that the state has a monopoly on jurisdiction and thus on the truth. But even people who understand this have a problem understanding how the organization of society without a state should proceed.

In this book I will therefore describe as specifically as possible what would happen if the state ceased to exist. Crime rates would fall dramatically. The Mafia and the deep state would disappear. The influential groups, both official and clandestine, would lose their power. Prosperity and social security would increase drastically.

This is a very important point: I will propose a number of specific solutions, but they originate from only one brain. In a natural order without states, however, millions of people and companies would work to solve such problems. This means that it is very likely that there will be much better answers to the questions described here.

I'm just here to give you some ideas. Always remember: If you can think of a better solution, you could start a business or a non-profit organisation yourself. If you don't feel able to do it yourself, you could hand the idea on. But you can be quite sure that someone else is already working on the solution. If a problem really exists, there is also a demand for the solution. There would be no state that could prevent this solution, as it is already doing today in countless places.

Many thanks to Michael Burtscher (NU ART) for the cover design. Special thanks to Johanna von Bogen for everything she has done for me and to Naomi Seibt, who came up with the English title.

Note: Links to further information on the several topics can be found in the Ebook. However, they are not necessary for any comprehension of the text.

Taking stock

Originally this was going to be a very long chapter. But the amount of information about something going badly wrong is so overwhelming that I don't even know where to start. There are now also many alternative media from which you can obtain information. But since these keep disappearing repeatedly thanks to increasing censorship, I will not refer to specific media. On my website you will always be kept up to date. Even if it is turned off, I will reinstall it elsewhere.

But I want to give you some clues. Due to the "refugee crisis", many people probably think that one only has to solve this problem, and everything will be fine again. That's fundamentally wrong. Germany was already on the brink of collapse. When, for example, the billions of euros of money in the state-run euro experiment finally become due, Germany will already plunge into chaos. Even before the refugee crisis, we had a rampant crime problem that has been covered up for decades.

For example, for a long time now only a fraction of the break-in cases are solved. The clear-up rate has been well below twenty percent for years. The state praises itself for a higher clear-up rate of other crimes because it determines for itself whether a crime has taken place at all. If a murder is discarded as a natural death or accident, for example, this crime does not appear in any statistics.

On my website you will find, for example, a number of cases in which corpses have appeared where, according to the police, "no external influence" was found. Some of the cases are so hair-raising that the possibility of external influence is excluded even in cases of corpses lacking a head. In individual cases there may be an explanation, but the mass of findings speaks for itself.

How on earth could the monopolist be trusted? He alone determines what information is made public. Often there is not even an explanation given for what is supposed to have happened. This is, of course, in the interest of the state, because then it doesn't have to do anything and can also distract from its own failure and that of politics.

Another example of how rarely justice is served can be found in the area of sexual crimes. In the German federal state of Brandenburg, ruled by a coalition of Social Democrats, Greens and the Left Party, 2,423 reported sexual offences only led to only 78 convictions. That's a ridiculous three-percent quota. In addition, the number of unreported cases of sexual offenses is particularly high. To a not inconsiderable extent, this is due to how the victims are treated. That would be quite different in a private law society (abbreviated: PLS; also called private law order), as you will see presently. But the low rate of convictions alone means that fewer and fewer crimes are reported, because the victims rightly say that there is nothing gained from it, except for trouble, wasted time and expense.

We must also take into account that even supporters of the "constitutional state" admit that the official statistics are doctored. So writes "Die Welt" on 24 January 2016:

That was January 11th. Wendt and Kraft were guests of the ARD political talk "Hart aber fair". And the trade unionist replied to the head of state government by describing a "Germany-wide phenomenon": a minister of the interior need not decree anything "because every police officer knows that he has to fulfil a certain political expectation which is infused". Everyone knows the "tricks of the trade", such as simply describing Sinti and Roma as "people with frequently changing places of residence".

"Better not say anything, then you can't do anything wrong," Wendt said. The trade unionist also blamed this "expectation" on the fact that the Cologne police had not communicated or played down the events of New Year's Eve.

If officials do name the perpetrators clearly, they immediately get muzzled:

On June 19 2015, the Dortmund police issued a press release warning the population of the increased activities of these confidence tricksters — and formulated an indication of origin. In this case it was about "situations in which (mostly North African) young men are on the street ... who 'dance up' to selected victims, distract them in such a way as to then steal wallets or mobile phones.

Four weeks later, a letter from the federal authority arrived in Dortmund. In it, the Anti-Discrimination Agency ADS described it as questionable whether the press release was in accordance with the guidelines of the police in the state of NRW. "There is a danger that these groups of people in the population will be placed under general suspicion as a result", the ADS reminded in the letter seen by "Die Welt", and first reported on by

"Focus". It goes on to say: "We suggest that the reference to North African origin be deleted from the press release. "

The Dortmund police, however, did not stand by their statement and revised their own assessment.

The "HAZ" quotes a State Office of Criminal Investigations (LKA) official on November 19 2015:

"There are instructions to use our room for interpretation in such a way that civil peace is preserved," says Schwarz. The official complains that he's expected to play down and trivialize cases like the bloody brawl. Too much bad news from the refugee camps could upset the mood. The fear: Right-wing noisy troublemakers were only waiting for their prejudices to be confirmed and a boost for their ideological myopia. Schwarz remained silent for a long time. Now he thinks it's his duty to speak. "There's no lying, nothing is covered up, but things are deliberately left out. That's the problem," says Schwarz...

Recently, Schwarz reports, he sat face to face with his Home Secretary. It was about the preparatory work on police crime statistics, about the question of conspicuous delinquency in and around refugee centres. The population cannot be burdened with a result that confirms that there is an accumulation of sexual violence, of the most serious bodily harm. "That would be a bad result," Schwarz understood from the supreme employer.

That's what he passed on to his people. Then statistical filters would be set a little differently, some figures would be delivered late, things would be concealed, pushed away and renamed. The word "honor killing" doesn't appear in the reports. In German police diction, many things can be wrapped up, not wrongly, but also without corners and edges. "We use the room for interpretation to preserve civil peace." Schwarz is often tormented by enormous pangs of conscience. "You have to use your discretion so that you don't lie, but the sensation seekers don't get a foothold." But the cold truth of statistics is glossed over.

Even with the burglary figures, where the clear-up rate is already so low according to official figures, falsification takes place. This is what the WAZ writes on January 11 2017:

The Oberhausen police leadership did not present the complete number of cases to the citizens, but only a small excerpt. This is particularly fatal in the case of the often-discussed break-ins in the urban area. The number of burglaries is almost twice as high as the officially presented crime statistics of the Oberhausen police.

In many places the constitutional state has already capitulated. In England, the police chief is seriously suggesting that paedophiles no longer be arrested because there are so many, the BBC reported on February 28 2017. No policeman at all can be found in so-called no-go areas anywhere in Europe.

"Die Welt" reports on January 28 2016 that "minor crimes" committed by refugees are no longer investigated at all:

In Kiel, refugees without identity papers or official registration are not prosecuted for simple offenses such as shoplifting or damage to property. As the "Kieler Nachrichten" reports, the leadership of the Kiel Police Headquarters and the public prosecutor's office had agreed this at the beginning of October 2015, according to an internal police report.

The „Bild-Zeitung" had already reported on a guideline issued by the Police Headquarters in Kiel, which instructed police officers to pursue smaller crimes against refugees less intensively.

Accordingly, the instruction of October 2015 states that in the case of simple offenses such as shoplifting and damage to property, "a personal identification procedure or treatment by the identification service" should regularly be cancelled. This would apply if the personal details of the refugees could not be clearly established or could not be clarified within twelve hours.

The reason given for the order was that the costs were too high compared with the prospects of success.

The German Federal Criminal Police Office BKA report also uses tricks. In the report, officials have unceremoniously deducted more than 600,000 "refugees" when recording criminal offences.

The chaos is now so great that the various institutions of the constitutional state are attacking each other. At the same event where police unionist Rainer Wendt was pointing the finger at politicians, the defense lawyer and Professor Ulrich Sommer was attacking the police, as "Focus" writes on November 24 2017:

The most provocative theses of the evening did not come from the very defensive Rainer Wendt, but from his interlocutor on the podium, the defence lawyer and Professor Ulrich Sommer. The latter went so far as to say that being a policeman was probably the "most indecent profession".

According to Sommer, policemen would "fudge" criminal files and thus "manipulate" the courts. He has already seen a lot of "lying police officers in court," Sommer adds. The police officers obviously no longer understand their role in the constitutional state, according to the defense lawyer. And: "The courts are not the extended arm of the police. "

To top it all, the event was disturbed by left-wing extremists, who prefer to have even fewer police and even more migrants.

Professional police and justice associations complain about an acute shortage of personnel according to a Reuters report of August 2 2017:

The nation was short of at least 2,000 judges and public prosecutors as well as 20,000 police officers, the German Judges' Association and the Police Union declared on Wednesday in Berlin. This was having a direct impact on security. Public prosecutors' offices and courts were more and more frequently resorting to discontinuing proceedings. "Of the five million completed criminal proceedings, one third were terminated in 2015 with or without restraints," said Jens Gnisa, chairman of the Judges' Association. Ten years earlier, the quota had been a quarter.

Especially alarming was the release of highly suspect people from pre-trial detention if proceedings lasted too long. "This happens between 40 and 45 times a year at the moment," said Gnisa. These are suspects who are accused of serious criminal offenses. The judicial system is jammed at every turn. "I also have the feeling that the citizens realise this more and more and have doubts about the security in their country. "In addition to criminal justice, the administrative courts, which have to deal with the large number of asylum proceedings, are particularly burdened. Due to the upcoming wave of retirements, the situation in the judiciary and police will become even worse in the next ten to 15 years.

Even the above-mentioned president of the Judges' Association, Jens Gnisa, "despairs of the legal system" and has written a book entitled "Das Ende der Gerechtigkeit" ("The End of Justice"). In fact, there is a fundamental mistake in the system, which I will explain to you now:

The real root of evil

If you want to solve a problem, you have to recognize the cause. It is important to really get to the heart of the matter. If one doesn't recognize the true cause, one will only ever treat the symptoms.
It will surprise some libertarians that I don't see the true cause of social and economic problems in the violation of property rights, the principle of non-aggression or natural law.

The non-observance of these principles is only the consequence of the violation of another principle. When we discover this principle, we have discovered the root cause of the problem. If we know the root cause, all problems can be traced back to this principle. If this isn't possible, we have not found the root cause at all. The real root cause can be summed up in ten dry words:

The conflict solver must not be party to the conflict.

In other words:

The one who adjudicates a conflict, i.e. the judge, must not himself be part of the conflict.

That's immediately obvious. Imagine you thought a company had sold you a faulty product. If it accepts the product back, out of goodwill or insight, no conflict arises. If the company refuses to return the money to you, it would obviously be nonsensical to have the company decide who is in the right in this instance.

The State is by definition the ultimate judge in all legal matters, including those concerning itself. This can't work at all. For example, you cannot complain with the aim of getting your taxes back if politicians do not keep their election promises or if you generally think that the state is not doing what you expect it to do.

It was Hans-Hermann Hoppe, for me the most important living philosopher and one of the greatest in history, who discovered and brilliantly worked out this principle as the basis for libertarianism. Most anarchists acknowledge this principle, but often mistakenly believe that this is only an extension of libertarianism or the Austrian School. It would just be another arrow in the quiver to shoot at state enthusiasts.

In reality, Hoppe has discovered something completely new that has taken the theory to a whole new level. The Austrian School remains useful to describe the consequences of limited property rights. However, this principle is independent of the Austrian School or Libertarianism and precedes the right of ownership. I'll try to prove that to you logically:

There's no property in a state. There exists only property by grace of the state, so-called fiat property. Not only does the state levy taxes, it can also take away already guaranteed property rights at any time and does so regularly. The state determines, for example, that the owner of an apartment may not leave it empty, for example because it wants to accommodate so-called refugees in it. The state even has the audacity to speak of "misappropriation" when you rent out your own apartment to tourists. In Munich there is a fine of 500,000 euros for doing this. The state can introduce a wealth tax overnight or even the taxation of air — see the proposals on the CO2 tax.

It follows logically from this that there is either no property at all or only if there is no state. I will subsequently call this state, the final decision-maker or ultimate judge for conflicts, a monopolist on the use of force. The term is not quite clear-cut, because the citizen may use violence for self-defense, for example, but in the end the state decides whether this use of violence was lawful. Therefore, I use this term because it is common and not as bulky as "ultimate judge in a particular territory". I'll show you that property actually exists. Then all that remains is a logical conclusion:

If the absence of a monopolist on the use of force is the prerequisite for property rights, it means that the emergence of property is only the *result of* the absence of an ultimate judge.

Thus we have discovered the basic principle for solving human conflicts and thus also the basic cause for the emergence of property. This view — apart from being true — has several advantages:

First, apparent contradictions in problems that are controversial even among libertarians, such as the absolute validity of property rights or the controversial question of what it means when it is said that the discoverer of unowned property "mixes" his labor with it, dissolve.

Second, it relieves us of the need to debate philosophical or moral questions. State enthusiasts like to argue about concepts. Left-wing state enthusiasts, for example, claim that it would be aggression against them if they had to work at low wages. Opponents of natural law present it as if it were the law of the strongest. Others, on the other hand, question the right to one's own body by saying that one is only the occupier, not the owner of one's body. There are always good arguments against this, but if we stick to the basic principle we have discovered, the discussion of these questions is of secondary importance.

No one can deny that the judge can't be part of the conflict. Even if someone denied it, you could say to him:

"Well, we have a conflict here. I suggest I decide who's right." If your counterpart concedes, you decide you're right. If he refuses this concession, you have proven that the conflict decision maker can't at the same time be a party to the conflict.

The fact that this principle *precedes* property rights also becomes clear in other ways. The state cannot only take away your material property from you, it can also gain complete control over your body. When the state locks you up and ties you up, not only do you no longer have a chance to benefit from the fruits of your labor, you are de facto no longer even the owner of your body. You can't move because you're tied up — in a straitjacket, for example.

It goes even further: the state can even forbid you to argue that you own your body. It can literally shut you up. In fact, that's exactly what it does regularly. Immigration or Islam critics are currently being sentenced one after the other to severe punishments, including prison sentences, while at the same time foreign rapists are running free.

The state generally forbids "anti-state propaganda". Every anarchist is by definition an enemy of the state. The main reason why not all anarchists are in prison is that there are still too few to be considered dangerous by the state. But totalitarian regimes have always imprisoned anarchists. And the state is becoming more and more totalitarian, as even the most naïve and ignorant citizen should have recognized by now.

Let us therefore state that the absence of a monopolist on the use of force is not only a prerequisite for property, it is even a prerequisite for being able to argue for one's right to self-ownership. It should now be clear that we have discovered the basic principle by means of which we can deal with all socially relevant issues of human conflict.

If you're good at thinking abstractly, you can stop reading at this point. Once you have identified the root cause, you can derive everything yourself. It is certainly no coincidence that people with a very high IQ are demonstrably advocating libertarian principles. A survey among members of the Triple Nine Society (the link to the original report has now disappeared, but was still there at the time of printing my previous book), who must be smarter than 99.99 percent of the population, showed that they support libertarian principles in all matters. This is because they are better able to think abstractly than the rest of the population and are immediately aware, for example, of the negative consequences of regulation.

Take the test: Present this chapter to someone who has an IQ of 130 or higher. They will probably say immediately that the remarks are correct and that the state must be abolished. They may also have to read the rest of the book and other literature if they haven't dealt with the subject before at all. If they're still in favor of the state after that, let them show you their test results. If they actually show a high IQ, send them into a public debate with me. I'm looking forward to it.

Libertarian Issues: Some Lifeboat Scenarios

Before we investigate actual practice, I would like to briefly address a few issues that are controversial even among libertarians. State enthusiasts like to construct so-called "life boat" scenarios in order to put anarchists argumentatively on the back foot. These are characterized by the fact that they are completely unrealistic and hardly ever occur in practice. But if I'm going as far as claiming to have discovered the basic principle, I would also like to support my case on the basis of particularly difficult scenarios.

One question that is controversial even among libertarians is that of the appropriation of unowned land. Among libertarians and all other rational people it's undisputed that only the first person who discovers the property can appropriate it without conflict. That's why it belongs to the first person who finds it. But how big can this property be? How far do its external borders extend?

In addition, here's a classic lifeboat scenario: A ship sinks and the occupants save themselves on a lonely island that doesn't yet belong to anyone. There is necessarily exactly one person who was the first to discover the island. Suppose he manages to be the first one to swim to the island. Does he own the whole island now? Let's also assume that he had such a big lead that he quickly built a rudimentary fence around the island, for example from ship ropes or lianas.

The classic libertarian answer is: he must mix his labor with the land. It wasn't enough just to build a fence. He must therefore at least make it clear that, for example, he wants to cultivate the arable land and start farming it. But how much time does he have? What percentage of the land does he have to manage and when? I admit that this question has occupied me for a long time and I was quite glad that state enthusiasts so rarely dare to discuss with me. Therefore no one had asked me this question publicly.

But with the realization that the decisive factor is not the property but the absence of a monopolist on the use of force, the difficulties of this question disappear into thin air. So let's say the rest of the crew arrives on the island. Surely no one would accept that the first would own the entire island. Someone would suggest letting a neutral person decide the matter. Possibly the captain of the ship is well liked and they would agree on him. Perhaps the second-in-command or someone else has proved to be particularly fair on the journey so far and is left to decide. Probably he would decide that the first one could choose a plot and the others in turn (either by arrival or by rank or by lot) can choose other plots.

This is what's crucial: The squabblers have agreed beforehand on a judge. I'll explain later what basically happens if people don't come to an agreement. For this scenario it is only important to recognize this: There is no absolute property right that magically falls from the sky; it is instead the result of a decision-making process.

The matter will become even clearer if we introduce the state at this point. For example, if the castaways were British nationals, Britain would certainly insist that this island now belongs to the United Kingdom. And the state, as we know, would probably argue that only large companies, those that already have the greatest influence on the state, would be able to develop this island. The state would grant concessions and the law firms of these companies would write the rules.

Whether the first discoverers get anything of this cake, and how much, is in the hands of the state. It is obvious that whatever results from this is very likely worse for the occupants of the boat than what the judge appointed by the team decides.

Another scenario that – as far as I remember – was raised in a Skype discussion between a state advocate and the anarchist Walter Block is the following:

Imagine if you'd gotten lost in the woods and were close to dying of thirst. You see a fenced property with a spring. The question the proponent of the state asked was: Would you drink from it? As far as I remember, Block avoided the question and came back to basic questions. But the advocate of the state made his point: You would, in the end, drink from it. What is a system worth if you would not abide by the rules yourself (the inviolability of property)?

My answer would have been: The rules are part of the game, as is the sanction for non-compliance with the rule. Example: In the semi-final of the 2002 World Cup, Michael Ballack of the German team slide-tackled an opponent player, received the red card and missed the final (If Mehmet Scholl hadn't stayed at home as a possible replacement, making his girlfriend happy, Germany would probably have won the World Cup). Ballack knew he was risking a red card, but it was worth more to him to stop the opponent. If Ballack had kicked someone in the street, he'd be punished for assault. This means that the fact that I myself violate a rule does not mean that I generally reject it. But I have to be ready to face the consequences.

Let's take the example further: Let's assume that the thirsty person climbs over the fence and drinks from the spring. The owner gets his shotgun and shoots at him. For simplicity's sake, we assume that he survived and brings the owner before a neutral court. How would a neutral judge decide? We're assuming someone happened to film everything.

If it were clear that the owner could see that the intruder was unarmed and had shot him in the back without warning, he would certainly not acquit him. Basically, it strengthens the owner's position if he puts up signs everywhere saying that entering is forbidden and every intruder will be shot. This does not mean, however, that — without state laws — neutral judges who are respected by many would allow everything. Let me give you an example:

Suppose a bunch of criminals are about to storm your property. Your neighbor stands next to you with a gun in his hand, but refuses to help you. You step onto his property, snatch his weapon, shoot at the attackers and repel them. Now, if your neighbor sued you in a private lawsuit, would a judge convict you of theft? Certainly not. He would probably sentence you to replace the cartridges and possibly a payment for the wear and tear of the rifle, but he would certainly not punish you for stealing or stepping on someone else's property.

The same applies, by the way, if, for example, you crossed this property to save a woman from being raped — assuming there was no other way to get to her. If the neighbor shot you in the back while crossing his property, although he could clearly see that you were not attacking him, but only trying to help, the neighbor would certainly be convicted. The same would be true if you tried to help your drowning son, who had entered the neighbor's swimming pool without permission.

In reality, such scenarios are unrealistic because all those involved would have voluntarily subjected themselves to certain rules, but we will come to that in a moment. My point here is to show that property is not something absolute that somehow falls from the sky. This is by no means to be confused with relativism, for there is an absolute rule: namely that the judge must not be part of the conflict.

Had the castaways recognized this, they would have had the idea that the judge was also part of the conflict, because he would certainly have liked to have a plot of land on the island as well. The perfect solution would have been to exclude this, and instead to pay him a respectable wage for his work as a judge, so that he voluntarily renounced a plot of land, or to promise him a certain plot of land as a wage beforehand.

In the following I will call the underlying principle, that the conflict decision maker must not be a conflict party, the *principle of the neutral judge.*

What about those who don't subject themselves to rules?

The question that everyone rightly asks is, who enforces the rules without the state? What about those who don't sign contracts, but just roam the area robbing and pillaging?

First of all, it should be noted that there are exactly three cases that need to be taken into account. In a private law system, competing companies would provide security. To protect their property, most people would insure themselves, but probably not all. It is therefore important to distinguish between three cases where two people are involved in a conflict:

1. Both are insured. This will be the rule and is also the easiest to treat.
2. One person is insured, the other isn't.
3. Neither person is insured.

Re 1: If both are insured, they have previously agreed to certain rules. In principle, these rules can be reduced to just one: You must not steal. Considering the body as one's property, this includes not hurting or killing anyone. Nothing else makes sense.

Re 2: There is a view, especially among voluntarists (actually voluntaryists), that a murderer who prior to his deed didn't sign a contract agreeing not to murder cannot be imprisoned because this violates the right of property or the principle of non-aggression. I think this view is completely absurd. Some voluntarists and also some libertarians think that these people would simply be ostracised and could not move freely without insurance. This is certainly partly true, but they would still be locked away, as I will show presently.

The reason for this view may be precisely that the representatives of this view don't understand the root cause of the problem. They seem to believe that the observance of the principle of non-aggression or property rights somehow fall from the sky. Property rights would arise because most people would believe in these principles once they have been explained to them. In my opinion, this assumption is fundamentally wrong and also a reason why many supporters of the state ask themselves how the whole thing would actually work.

We can see that almost nobody believes in property rights, because almost everyone supports the state. Now one could argue that this is because nobody explains it to them. First, it is impossible to explain it to everyone, and second, the state is doing everything it can to avoid explaining it to anyone. Thirdly, there are countless people who do not accept this point of view, even after it has been explained to them a hundred times.

No, property rights don't arise from the conviction of people that they exist. They arise automatically when there is no monopolist on the use of force. Let us imagine the following scenario:

From one day to the next, the state abolishes itself. All insurers simultaneously come up with the idea of offering people the following contract: You can steal from whomever you want, and we will support you. Immediately, the insured would start stealing from each other. Even the most successful thieves would be constantly robbed, because it is allowed. It is immediately obvious that this makes no sense — not even for a thief. Already by the next day all insurers would change and offer the only rule that makes sense: We protect you from being robbed, and you agree not to steal.

So we see again: the right to property arises because competing companies have to offer their customers a useful product. The monopolist on the use of force doesn't have to. That's why he steals. It's simple. In the following I will refer to the non-aggression principle and property rights by the latter term, since both mean the same thing anyway: Nobody is allowed to initiate violence, i.e. to be the first to use it to injure someone or take something away.

But what about those who do not take out insurance? It's simple: they won't have anyone to protect them. So if an uninsured thief steals from an insured person, the insurance intervenes and ensures that the thief is arrested and taken to court.

This does not violate the principle of non-aggression, because the thief has already committed aggression against the property, but that's not the point. The market is not interested in abstract principles, morality or philosophy. It just works. What's important for you is this: The abstract principle of the neutral judge does not need to be understood by anyone. This principle automatically ensures that it works. Just as failure to follow the principle automatically ensures that the monopolist on the use of force steals — precisely because he is the ultimate judge. As you can see, we can always trace everything back to this one basic principle without having to conduct moral, philosophical or natural law discussions.

Then couldn't an insured person just punish the thief or the killer himself? Theoretically, yes. But in practice, an insurer would insist on being involved in such cases. After all, he is liable for the customer and therefore wants to ensure that everything is done properly. Firstly, the victim cannot know for sure whether the thief is insured, and secondly, not being insured does not mean that you cannot sue. We'll see that in the next case:

Re 3: A steals from B. Neither is insured. What can B do? Well, B simply hires a security firm to track A down, arrest him, and bring him before a neutral court. The fact that B is not insured only means that he must pay upfront. In the end, when A is sentenced, he must not only pay for the damage, but also for the costs of his capture and sentencing. More about that later.

But couldn't A in turn hire a security company to protect him? You must understand that although it's possible not to insure yourself as an individual, it's completely impossible for companies to act if they are uninsured. An entrepreneur has to hire employees, use roads, rent rooms, buy weapons and so on. For all these actions he needs insurance, as I will explain with further examples. This insurer will of course require that the security company only prosecutes (potential) criminals and not blameless people who adhere to the rule of not stealing.

But couldn't A turn to a mafia company that doesn't have insurance because it's already trying to steal from everyone? As I will show later, such organizations disappear from the market simply because it wouldn't be profitable and they wouldn't be able to move within civilization anyway. Furthermore, in a state I can also turn to the mafia, except that it is usually identical with the state, i.e. the monopolist on the use of force, or is at least obviously not effectively combated.

So we see that even for uninsured people property rights arise simply because there is no monopoly on the use of force. And all for free! Socialists should like that! Briefly about the free-rider problem: it would practically not exist because it would be much more economical to insure oneself. Those who nevertheless didn't take out an insurance would be considerably limited in their opportunities to participate in civilized life.

A single assumption

After having theoretically proven that a monopolist on the use of force is unsuitable for resolving conflicts, the question arises as to what an anarchistic legal and prosecution system might look like in practice. It has to be said that it is very difficult to predict specific market results. What can be said for sure is that competition increases the quality of performance and lowers the price. This means that security increases, the crime rate falls and so do prices.

However, it is difficult to predict exactly which structure the market will adopt and which concrete solutions will prevail. Understandably, however, people want to get an idea of how it could work. That's the purpose of this book. If you want to make predictions, the fewer assumptions you have to make, the easier it is. For the purposes of this investigation, I make only one assumption:

Companies want to make profits.

This is a very elegant assumption, because nobody would deny it, neither a right-winger, nor a libertarian, nor a leftist. For example, I don't make assumptions about how many people are good or bad. I will analyse the situation from a purely economic point of view. Of course, economics isn't everything. For example, people voluntarily behave generously. That's what happens in my scenarios as the icing on the cake.

The nice thing is: You can join in if you enjoy it. Simply put yourself in the position of an entrepreneur. When I describe a problem, first lean back and consider how you could solve it. Very important is this: The solutions I present here originate from only one brain. In reality, thousands of companies will compete for the best solution.

It is therefore likely that the market will find better solutions. You can also write to me via my website if you have an idea. Please don't expect me to answer, I'm getting over a hundred emails a day now. But if you write in the title of the mail "solution proposal for..." or "objection against...", I will surely read the mail.

If I find suggestions or objections of general interest, I will include them in future editions of this book or in videos or articles.

Figures, data, facts

If your heart sank into your boots during the previous chapters because you have to pay for security, I can reassure you. First of all, nothing in life is free. Even a net transfer recipient pays, though not in money, but with the restriction of his quality of life. Once in the clutches of the state, he must allow himself be harassed by it. He can be forced into one-euro jobs, for example, is a perpetual petitioner and is checked regularly. All for his own good, of course.

Some people prefer to live on transfer payments rather than work, but neither do they know the alternative. As I worked out in my book, New World Order exposed, we could all work a fraction of the time we have to today if the state did not cheat us of the fruits of our labour through the inflationary monetary system and high taxes. I am sure that many transfer recipients would prefer to do a job two or three hours a day and be integrated in society, for example by maintaining social contacts with other productive members of society and by being able to act quite differently from someone who only lives off other people's money. Today they are often dependent on transfers because the state destroys so many jobs that it is much more difficult to find a job. In a free market economy there is no involuntary unemployment. See also "Human Action" by Ludwig von Mises. At the end of the present book you will read more about it.

Regardless of this, most people have no idea how little the state spends on the security of its citizens. Rounded up, the German state spends about 1.6 percent of the gross national product (Eurostat, 2015: 0.7 percent for police, 0.2 percent for fire brigade, 0.4 percent for courts, 0.1 percent for prisons and 0.1 percent for public order) on internal security, i.e. for police and courts combined. That's only 600 euros per year, that's 50 euros per month per capita. The Nobel Prize winner Milton Friedman once estimated that the dissolution of a monopoly would cut the prices in half. That would be only 25 euros a month.

Even a beggar pays more in taxes today. He does not pay taxes on his income, but he pays not only the VAT on every purchase, but also the taxes of the company from which he buys his products, the taxes and social contributions of the employees, the insurance tax for the building of the shop, the eco- and energy tax on the electricity and so on and so forth. So if a beggar earns and spends about ten euros a day, 50 percent of that, 150 euros a month, will certainly go to the state. An employee in Germany pays about 70 percent of his income if all taxes and social security contributions are taken into account.

The German state spends about another one percent, i.e. 30 euros per month and citizen, on the military. In a global private law order, there would be no need for military spending, but even if there were still states, private defense costs would be much lower, as I will show. But let's assume for argument's sake in the following that the costs for security would be 80 euros per month even in a private law system. Virtually anyone can afford this, and no one would be forced to buy security services.

What remains is the fee for the use of the roads. Here, too, there is the great misconception that the state makes them available free of charge. Far from it. An example:

The private motorway operator Autostrade charges 56 euros for the 776 kilometre journey from Milan to Naples. If you assume an average fuel consumption of 7.9 litres per kilometre, you will consume 61 litres of petrol. At a petrol price of 152 cents per litre, 90 cents go directly to the state as taxes, which, at 55 euros, is almost exactly the price of the motorway provider. In addition, however, there is also motor vehicle tax, insurance tax, taxes on the purchase of the car, taxes and levies on the employees who produce the car and the road, and so on. Moreover, this is not even a free market price, because the state guarantees Autostrade an exclusive monopoly.

Motorways in a private law system are also not comparable to so-called public-private partnerships (PPPs). These are often a disaster, because the state always has a say and the taxpayers' money can be squandered (see e.g. the new Berlin Airport). If purely private providers go bankrupt, the losses are borne by the investor. The road can be sold and a more efficient company then operates the road. You can read more about how a private road system would be cheaper and more efficient in the work of Walter Block.

In addition, most roads would be "for free" in that they would be paid for by local residents. In private cities or so-called gated communities, the costs for the roads are simply included in the real estate prices. In addition, there is usually an annual maintenance fee, which is included in the ancillary costs.

So if you visit someone in such an area, the road is free of charge for you. And of course the quality is much better. Just compare any private road with the public one: it's as different as night and day. The reason for this, of course, is that suppliers want to attract customers, whether for an interregional road or for a residential project.

Whichever way you look at it, the cost of using roads is so low that it's of no consequence. Also, in a private law system you would only have the expenses that you consider necessary.

Anarchy in practice

In a private law system, for-profit companies would therefore take care of security. It is important to understand that the market tends toward division of labor (see the classic "I, Pencil" by Leonard E. Read) and specialization. For example, in Germany there are only four major car manufacturers, but hundreds of suppliers, each concentrating on what they do best. The situation would be similar in the security industry.

It is theoretically conceivable that a company could, for example, offer insurance against theft and at the same time the security team guarding your house or catching the criminals. However, it is extremely unlikely that this will prevail, because considerable conflicts of interest arise here (moral hazard). An insurer, for example, is interested in not paying out the sum insured. If the same company also conducts the investigation, there would be a risk that the results of the investigation would be manipulated in such a way that the amount paid out would be as low as possible. If, for example, the sum insured for suicide is low or — as a rule — zero, there is a tendency to declare a murder as suicide. The state does the same today because it then has no work and can enhance the statistics.

Another problem concerns the coordination of all the security groups. What if the criminal flees to a territory in which the company is not represented or only poorly represented? How would you solve this problem if you were an entrepreneur?

The Return of the Bounty Hunters

Economic action, in fact every action, is about incentives. So what should an incentive look like that solves the above problems? The solution lies in one word and that is actually just another term for incentive:

Reward.

In the not-so-wild West (see "The Not So Wild Wild West"), the problem of capturing criminals was efficiently solved by putting a price on their heads. Nowadays, the state also occasionally offers rewards for pertinent information.

This system could, however, be applied not only to the capture of perpetrators, but also to the investigation of criminal offences. I suggest the following method:

A insures himself against murder. If he dies, a certain sum is automatically made available for the clarification of the case. This money is paid to the person who solves the crime, if it is one. A company independent of the insurer, which is determined in advance by A, decides on the payout. Since only a tiny fraction of deaths are caused by murder, this insurance would be very cheap. Here is a numerical example:

A term life insurance policy of more than one million euros for a twenty-year-old over a period of twenty years costs about 25 euros a month (see comparison portals). However, out of 925,000 deaths in Germany, only 373 were classified as murder in 2015. The figure is certainly too low because the state has an incentive to assume a natural cause of death because it then doesn't have to investigate. But as you can see, in so few cases this is of no consequence. Even if all 10,000 suicides were considered murder, the numbers would be very low.

Assuming ten thousand murders, insurance against murder cost one percent (10,000/925,000) of 25 euros, or 0.25 euros. If we take the official homicide rate, we get one cent per month! So you see, it's about ridiculous amounts. They could also provide ten million euros for the investigation. Then according to official figures it would be ten cents, after actual murders perhaps twice as much.

How much does the state spend today to solve crimes? In 2016, 6.4 million crimes were recorded. For police and justice, the state spends 1.6 percent of the GDP of 3.1 trillion euros, i.e. just under 50 billion euros, i.e. 7,750 euros per crime. For murder investigation (and complex economic crimes) certainly the most is spent per case. But as you can see, ten million euros per murder is easily enough.

The reward system, however, has an interesting effect, which leads to far more being spent than the sum awarded. From an econometric point of view, one would assume that the sum of the expenses at the end would roughly correspond to the reward offered, minus the return customary in the industry. But that's just an idealized model. In practice, newcomers who want to make a name for themselves, for example by solving a case, are always pushing their way onto the market.

They might even be willing to spend more than the ten million just to get publicity.

It's hard to tell where the optimal point is. Possibly private detective agencies would spend up to ten percent to get the total amount. Companies that regularly miscalculate withdraw from the market. But the decisive factor is this: the ten million (or whatever sum) will always remain there, or for as long as previously agreed. This is the basis for the premium. However, as these are paltry amounts, the term of the contract will be as long as possible.

So let's suppose that a number of detective agencies have spent money and at some point they all give up because the evidence of a crime has not solidified. Suddenly a new clue appears. Part of the money would always be made available for relevant information from the population, so that there should be no lack of informants. A new witness could turn up, a fake suicide note, a false alibi, and so on. No matter how much was spent before, suddenly there is an incentive to investigate further.

The agencies which had already spent a lot of money now have the incentive to save their investment and have a knowledge advantage through the information already collected. They could also resell this information in order to recoup part of their investment. But a newcomer could also start from scratch, because with this new clue the risk/reward ratio has improved considerably.

It is also possible for contracts with agencies to be drawn up in such a way that they have to share the information with the contracting authority (which decides on the payment), whereby it is difficult to prevent an agency from withholding information.

But whichever way you look at it, there is an enormous economic incentive to clear up the case.

Compare that with today's situation. Today, a single state prosecutor decides how to deal with the case. The case is being investigated by low-paid police officers working overtime who have no economic interest in the case. They can't be fired unless they commit a crime themselves, they also keep their job if they simply work to rule and thus have a cushy job. That doesn't mean that there are no cops who do their very best.

But the frustration, especially of the policemen, is growing thanks to politics. If they catch a criminal and he is also a migrant, he is usually immediately released anyway or gets a ridiculously low penalty. Alone the news section of my website shows hundreds of such cases. And that's just the tip of the iceberg being released to the public.

The rewards system also explains who catches the perpetrators. Part of the money is always set aside for the perpetrator's capture. So every security firm in a private law system has an interest in catching criminals. In addition, they naturally want to protect their customers, because otherwise they lose their orders. Nothing would be more embarrassing for a security company than a wanted criminal staying in your region and then robbing a customer.

Now you put yourself in the position of a criminal of today and tomorrow. In what world would you rather be a criminal? In today's world, where an overworked, poorly paid police inspector is in charge of you and the penalties are ridiculously low, or tomorrow's world, where hundreds of detective agencies hunt you down to get the reward that is on your head?

I think you'd quit your "job" as a criminal pretty quick. This is exactly what I mean when I write above that when a monopoly is abolished the quality increases and the price decreases.

Another aspect is that poor people in particular would benefit enormously from such a system. Let's take a beggar as an extreme case. He does not have to insure himself against theft, because he lives from hand to mouth. If someone steals his begging bowl, he has to beg longer the next day, doesn't eat anything one day or goes to a food assistance center.

Perhaps he also has no great interest in taking out insurance against murder, because he already possesses a certain fatalism as a beggar. In a civilized world in which there are no Islamists running around slaughtering "infidels", there is hardly any economic reason to kill him. But private aid organizations might have an interest in insuring him. Since it costs only a few cents, they could insure him in addition to the soup they give him. For example, he would only have to leave a fingerprint.

The interesting thing is now: if he dies, there is suddenly an economic interest in solving the case. Today, neither the police nor the general public care much when a beggar dies. But a private detective agency does, because it gets the reward, no matter who it is. The aid organisation also has an interest in giving relevant advice, because then a part of the reward beckons, which in turn can be spent on charitable causes. But the beggar is only an extreme case.

Basically, poor people don't have a big lobby. However, since the insurance is so inexpensive, it is guaranteed that private detective agencies will also want to solve such cases. Ten million euros is ten million euros.

If you are a crime thriller fan, you will probably immediately have the idea that this would be an incentive to have the beggar murdered and then solve the case in order to get the reward. But this is only paid out if the murderer is caught, and he would surely be the first to testify who gave him the order in exchange for a lesser penalty. In addition, the insurance company has an interest in not paying out, and would conduct counter-investigations if something seemed suspicious to it.

But in principle it is very important to examine what conflicts of interest would arise in such a system and how they could be avoided.

The moral temptation: possible conflicts of interest

I have already pointed out in my previous books that contractual relations are examined with the help of the principal-agent theory. But I will try to avoid technical terms. In the end, it is always about the fundamental possibility of conflicts of interest with regard to contracts.

In the case of a reward for investigating a crime, for example, the insurance company has an interest in not paying the sum. But you should keep in mind, with everything you are reading now, that it is very risky for a company in the free market to behave badly towards its customers. Competitors always have an interest in uncovering deficiencies among their rivals.

The state, on the other hand, remains no matter how much injustice it does. Therefore, the number of scandalous verdicts in a state is in principle many times higher than in a private law system. All you have to do is open the newspaper on any given day. And then you wonder if that judge or that policeman would have kept his job in a free market.

A truly free market not only produces better performance due to competition, it also finds better rules. In this case, it would be immediately clear that the company that decides on the payment of the reward has a special position of power. This would be clear to all professional contract partners. For example, the paying company would of course have to insure itself and thus subject itself to certain rules.

Both the reinsurers of the company paying out insurance and the insurance companies of the investigating detective agencies would then have the right to carry out a kind of audit and, for example, to inspect the evidence and communication with the other contracting parties.

If there were any inconsistencies, the company could be replaced. The security comes into the system because the detectives have an interest in the payment and the insurance company does not. The company that decides on the pay-out in turn derives its reputation from the fact that it acts in a fair and balanced manner.

I will deal with the fundamental problem of corruption in the following section on court companies.

The neutral judge

How then are neutral court companies selected? Let us first consider the simplest case when both the plaintiff and the defendant are insured. First of all, both insurance companies will try to find an amicable solution because this will save court costs. If both plaintiff and defendant agree, the case is closed.

If one of the parties disagrees, they go to court. As a rule, the major insurers have already determined among themselves which portfolio of court companies they want to use. Depending on the case, it will be a local court and above all one that specialises in such types of cases. It will also have a reputation for fast turnaround and fair prices, as everyone involved has an interest in it.

You will already see a huge difference between this and state courts. Legal proceedings often drag on for months or even years. Firstly, because the monopolist doesn't care anyway, secondly, because he has no economic interest at all in a quick settlement, and thirdly, because the state basically works very inefficiently.

The customers usually don't notice anything about this, but let's assume that one of them doesn't want to accept the court at all and the parties to the dispute can't agree on one. A rule that could then be included in the contracts, for example, would be that the plaintiff could select any company from the portfolio of the defendant's insurer. The defendant has already agreed to this company. Since in the majority of all cases the plaintiff will already have a reason for his complaint, he should have the first choice.

In the next instance, for example, the defendant could then select a company from the plaintiff's portfolio. If this court company comes to the same conclusion, the defendant would have to accept the judgment, unless new evidence emerges.

Insertion: There would always be several instances because the insurers would be liable. If it turns out, for example, that someone has been incorrectly imprisoned for years, that would be very expensive. Therefore, there is in principle a great deal of interest in reaching a fair judgment, except in the case of a plaintiff suing out of pure malice. On the other hand, there are the interests of both insurers and the defendant.

So what if one of them doesn't have insurance? Of course, he can also voluntarily agree on a court company, which he will usually do. The more complicated he makes it for the other side, the more expensive it will be for him if he loses in the end. But let us assume that he does not accept any of the proposed companies and that he has not previously agreed to any portfolio.

Well, then he's out of luck. He is brought before a court proposed by the plaintiff's insurer. He doesn't have anyone to protect him. He cannot be a customer of a security company, which would have required him to take out insurance. In theory, he could retroactively commission a security company to do this, but this company would also be insured and its terms would certainly state that they should not retroactively protect someone who refuses to appear before any court. So the security company would have to start a war because of this one customer; nobody would do that of course.

Does that mean you'd now do whatever you want with that holdout? No, he will nevertheless be brought before a court with a good reputation, because it makes no economic sense to throw him in the dungeon just like that. There could be bad press, relatives and friends could sue. He himself may prove his innocence some day and so on.

If the court finds him guilty, he must serve his sentence. In prison, he can still try to prove his innocence. But it is quite clear that it is better to take out an insurance for a few bucks than to expose oneself to all these risks. This does not mean, however, that without insurance one would be basically without any rights.

Even in this case, this applies: All companies must pay attention to their reputation. If completely senselessly uninsured people who are actually innocent were locked away, there would surely be an outcry. These are typical lifeboat scenarios that will hardly occur in reality. As a rule, one of the two is really a criminal and the point is to prove it to him and to pronounce a punishment. If he has taken out insurance, the defense is a bit easier for him, but then again he has agreed in advance to the procedure and also the possible punishment.

Penalties in a private law system

What would penalties look like in a private law system? Quite simply, the penalties would be precisely calculated to minimize the number of crimes.

Some libertarians believe that a thief only has to return the stolen goods. That's complete nonsense, of course. Nobody would agree to such a regulation, because then it would be rational for everyone to steal, because in the worst case he only has to return what he has stolen, but in all cases where he is not caught he would make a profit. Now one could object that the libertarian who argues in such a crazy way would indeed agree to such an arrangement. But all mentally healthy people won't. There would be no insurance at all that would offer such a crazy arrangement (or would have such court companies in its portfolio) because it would then be constantly busy replacing stolen goods from criminals who had not been caught.

In any event, the thief would not only have to replace the stolen goods, he would also have to bear the costs of the proceedings, the investigation and arrest. The victim's insurance company wants their money back. But there would certainly be a penalty on top, which would depend on the severity of the crime. Here a particularly blatant example of how the German state handles this:

In April 2017, a 23-year-old Turk was acquitted on charges of rape, although the female (!) judge had no doubt about the victim's account. The perpetrator had clamped the victim's head between the metal struts of the bed and raped her for four hours, even though she fought back with her hands and feet. The perpetrator was acquitted because it was possible that with the "mentality of the Turkish culture" he could have mistaken the rape for wild sex.

That's complete nonsense, of course. It has to be understood that the state is not neutral even in cases where it could be theoretically neutral because it is not directly involved in the conflict. Judges are employees of the state and therefore follow its ideology. In Germany in particular, there is undoubtedly an ideology that migrants belong to a species particularly worthy of protection, whose "culture" must be considered and who must therefore be handled with velvet gloves. Just take a look at the daily newspaper or my website. There are hundreds, if not thousands, of cases where migrants receive more lenient sentences than Germans.

The case isn't always as blatant as this one. But the tendency is so clear that even a liberal "Spiegel" journalist lost his rag when he once worked as a juror in a Berlin court and witnessed how migrants got away with ridiculous punishments. The Spiegel report can only be accessed with payment, so I quote from the article in the Wochenblick of 22 July 2017:

"I've seen more than a dozen cases (...) I've never seen a woman on trial. Always just men, young men. Most of them had what's called a migrant background.

Defendants are becoming more and more brutal.

Almost a quarter of all suspects are younger than 21. (...) Some have more entries in the criminal record than they can count years of life," is how Sven Böll describes his experiences at the Moabit Criminal Court, the largest criminal court in Europe. Last year, 16,000 (recorded!) crimes were committed per 100,000 inhabitants in Berlin. Predominantly by migrants.

"Assault, sexual abuse, extortion. Mostly they are straightforward criminal careers, with each case the defendants test themselves more and become a bit more brutal", writes Böll in his Spiegel report.

The state makes a fool of itself

"I can't believe it," writes the outraged left-wing journalist when he reports about a criminal from North Africa who has been released. He robbed and harassed defenceless people and led the court by the nose. As is customary among asylum seekers, he also stated a false age when entering the country, so that he would be sentenced according to the Juvenile Criminal Law.

Then the Spiegel man comes to the completely correct conclusion:

In the end, our state is also failing here.

But as you will gradually see, it is no coincidence that the state is failing here, but rather the compelling result of the fact that it has the monopoly on jurisdiction, for:

Do you really believe that there would be a single victim of rape who would accept a court company that would pass a sentence like that in the case of the brutal Turkish rapist?

Of course, in Germany there are left-wing female politicians who have been so degenerated by state re-education like those who have even apologized to their Arab-looking gang rapists. In a private law system she would of course be free to blow her rapists another one by way of an apology, but as in the theoretical case of the libertarian above, such an attitude would be the absolute exception and no insurance would offer such a tariff. Those who like to be raped by "refugees" do not insure themselves against it. All the others will insist on as much punishment as possible.

No one in their right mind would sign a contract that says: If the rapist comes from a "different culture", he is to be punished particularly mildly. Of course, the insurance company would have no incentive to offer such a feeble-minded regulation at all, because otherwise it would have to constantly pay legal costs and damages.

The above judge would have been dismissed immediately after such a scandalous decision and the decision would have been revised as soon as possible. Too great would be the danger for the court company never to get an assignment again. The judge might even have been held liable if the rapist had struck again before he could be taken into custody again. In a private law system, judges whose judgments are too often revised in the next instance would be sorted out anyway.

The market would decide through competition the rate of miscarriage of justice which is tolerable. Companies would try out what percentage minimizes the number of miscarriages, because their customers and insurance companies would hold them to account for that. For example, it may prove advantageous to dismiss all judges whose judgments are revised in more than ten percent of cases. It is impossible to predict where the optimal quota lies, but it is possible to predict that such a mechanism will certainly increase the quality of the judgments.

Compare this scenario with the current situation. The judge who released the Turkish rapist is still passing sentence today. She will probably even be promoted at some point (maybe even because of her scandalous verdict!). She gets her current salary and later her lavish pensions from taxes extracted from you, even from the rape victim!

Do you realize how this alone *must make* the quality of justice and security in a state almost infinitely worse than in a private law system?

How high would the penalties be: Since the victims and the insurances have an interest in as few crimes as possible, a penalty would arise that would deter enough offenders. After all, the criminal also makes an economic calculation that consists of two components: What is my risk of getting caught and what is my sentence?

As we have already seen, a private law system is much more efficient in identifying the perpetrators. That's a deterrent to a lot of criminals. If, however, the penalty were only to compensate for the damage, he would still have a positive expected value. So the punishment must be severe. As a rule, the courts will be local institutions. Although they may belong to a larger company, they adapt to local conditions. If rape is a major problem in a particular area, the penalties will be gradually increased until the problem is resolved.

It should be borne in mind that there are no written laws. The court companies that prevail are the ones that pronounce meaningful punishments. But wouldn't in that case even the smallest crime be eventually punishable by the highest penalty? No. There are several reasons for that:

First, it makes no economic sense to lock everyone away forever. Here is a figure: The gross domestic product per capita in Germany is around 40,000 euros. In other countries and in a PLS it is even much higher because the state does not restrict the economy (as one sees by tendency also with the states with a higher GDP). After 40 working years, a German has generated about 1.6 million euros. The exact figure doesn't matter, it's about the dimension. So every human being is a walking safe-deposit box, as long as he does not become a criminal.

So most companies have an interest in giving people a second chance to integrate into society. It is also important to the victim or his insurance company, because the perpetrator must bear the costs of the proceedings. On the victim's compensation: In a state, the victim gets virtually nothing and even has to pay taxes for the proceedings and the accommodation of the perpetrator. In a PLS, customers insure themselves for a certain compensation.

Specifically, the German legal system dates back to a time when people were still dueling. Therefore, crimes against life and limb are punished far too leniently in relation to property crimes (especially tax evasion, which is actually self-defense). Victims of violence, especially rape, often suffer for a lifetime. The sum insured would be correspondingly high. It could be a million euros for rape. The amount would probably not be arbitrarily high, because otherwise the incentive would be extremely high to fake a rape (more about that presently), but the compensations would certainly be much higher than today.

This sum is initially paid by the insurance company. But with such large sums, it cannot be assumed that every criminal can muster them. If there is no chance of ever paying it off, there is little incentive to become honest again. The market process will reveal at what threshold people are ready to become honest again.

The insurance company could, for example, agree contracts with the convicted person with corresponding clauses. For example, he has the choice of giving up a certain part of his income for repayment or alternatively languishing in prison for longer.

One possibility, for example, is "forced labour" in prison. In reality, there is no forced labour. You can force someone to do a certain job for eight hours, but you can't force them to do it well. He needs motivation for that. The best option would be piecework, i.e. an activity in which you settle on the basis of produced goods. The faster he works, the faster he gets out, for example, and can then repay the rest with honest work. Lifelong prisoners could be motivated with the easing of detention conditions. Better food, single cell, television and so on.

Anyone who comes out again and has not yet paid for everything would have to agree to surveillance, an electronic tag or something similar. The possibilities are almost endless. I'm just here to give you an idea of how it might work. The market process will reveal which rules are the most sensible.

However, it will not be the case, as I have occasionally read from libertarians, that the criminal can choose any luxury hotel as a prison, because then there would be no deterrent effect and the insured would not take part in that either. However, the penalties would be designed in such a way that on the one hand the number of crimes is minimized, but there is also the chance that the perpetrator becomes productive again.

A short excursion on the death penalty: Would there be one? Theoretically, yes, but I don't think so in practice. You must bear in mind that at least one insured person must agree to this penalty. So he'd have to sign off on the fact that if he was convicted, he'd be killed himself. Since almost everyone would probably be afraid of being wrongly convicted, most would probably forego this punishment.

But in one case it could be used. Take the crystal-clear case of a serial killer whose traces have been found on many victims. You would never let someone like that loose on society again. So how do you motivate him to work in prison? You could give him a choice of either working or being executed. Many more people would probably agree to such a regulation. Because innocent people would at least have the opportunity to strive for further revisions, all they would have to do is work.

In areas such as Europe, not even this would probably prevail, but for example in today's territory of the USA or other countries where approval of the death penalty is still high. Here, too, it should be borne in mind that a PLS would be much more efficient, i.e. there would be far fewer miscarriages of justice, for example because bad judges would be sorted out. In the case of harsh punishments, the burden of proof on a conviction would certainly also be higher. After all, here too the insurance company is liable for a miscarriage of justice.

My prognosis is that, over time, the death penalty would disappear completely, because crimes have become so rare because of increased efficiency they would simply no longer be an issue. With a PLS, a civilizing process automatically begins that generally leads to more peaceful behavior. More about that presently.

The biggest problems are regularly caused by so-called multiple offenders or repeat offenders. According to investigations by the German state criminal investigation offices, for example, a relatively small group of three to five per cent of young people who are repeat offenders are responsible for 30 to 60 per cent of criminal offences. The figures vary greatly depending on the federal state because crime rates are generally higher in large cities (source: Heinz Duthel, „Jugendkriminalität: Störung des Sozialverhaltens – Delinquenz - Intensivtäter").

If this problem were tackled, the number of crimes could be halved. If you consider that up to 50 percent of crimes are related to drugs, not only the use but also the sale of, procurement crime and violence in gang wars, you can already see what would be possible. In a private law system, there would be no victimless crimes. Buying drugs is a voluntary business.

Do you remember the 25 euros per month per citizen to which the contribution could fall if the monopoly were dissolved? Taking into account the elimination of drug-related crime and the control of repeat crime, we would be closer to less than ten euros. I don't want to gloss over this here, I just want to give you an idea of the immense potential savings.

In addition, even before mass immigration, 80 percent of intensive offenders in Berlin had a migration background. You already suspect what would be possible if this problem could be solved. Security would cost less than subscribing to a pay-TV channel or even a television journal. We will come to immigration in a moment, but fortunately the problem of repeat criminals is very easy to solve.

First, these guys (almost all of them male) don't seem to be very skilful, otherwise even the inefficient state wouldn't be able to catch them all the time. Second, we know exactly who they are.

In Bremen, for example, a Turkish repeat offender beat the son of a disabled woman unconscious in a dispute over a parking space. The fine gentleman had almost 200 crimes on his tally. The link has now been removed by the politically correct Radio Bremen in the left-green infested federal state, but numerous blogs refer with the same wording to it and on the URL you can see that there was this message. But you can search for similar cases yourself, it is however difficult because you need to know the exact number of crimes. But there are countless such cases.

It is unthinkable that such people would still be free in a private law system. As I have already explained, one would certainly be gracious with first offenders, because there is an economic interest in it. Many young people test themselves and commit a minor crime once. They usually stop when they get caught. In the case of shoplifting, for example, the most they get is a warning if the parents settle the damage and promise improvement. The shame of having been caught is enough for most people, especially when it comes to a court case after all.

Even the second time a neutral judge would probably turn a blind eye, but by the third time at the latest he knows that he is not dealing with a valuable member of society anymore. What happens then? First of all:

In a private law system, of course, it would be precisely registered who has committed a crime. There would be a kind of common register such as the Schufa (the German credit bureau) for bank customers. However, this register could by no means be compared with today's Schufa. The Schufa is an organization of an oligopolistic banking system.

By granting a money monopoly, the state has created a central bank that allows the affiliated banks to create money out of nothing. If you don't want to be connected to this system, you will not receive a license at all. At the same time, countless regulations ensure that the market remains closed to newcomers. They must meet high capital requirements, the board must have many years of experience in banking, so already be part of the club and so on. Such a club can, of course, afford to treat customers like dirt, and Schufa behaves accordingly. For example, it awards minus points and demands money for requesting your own Schufa entry!

In the case of a criminal record, however, *all* companies in a truly free market have an interest in ensuring that this record reflects reality as closely as possible. The companies are therefore very interested in ensuring that there are no false entries that present potential customers too badly.

Nowadays it is hardly possible to revise one's Schufa entry, even if it is wrong. A "criminal offence Schufa" would naturally also have to insure itself and would be responsible for wrong entries. The Schufa just laughs at such liability. They do what they want. I know a few cases from my circle of acquaintances that would make your hair stand on end.

Here, too, the following applies: Should PRS-Schufa mess up, there will be a competitor who offers better data. If you don't believe that, start a better one yourself.

Back to the register in a PLS: It would probably result in a system in which companies would quickly recognize what kind of candidate they were faced with. Since most people have little interest in the fact that every security guard at the shopping center has their entire curriculum vitae at their disposal, there will be insured persons' cards with which they can roughly identify who they are, i.e. a kind of traffic light system. Green means, for example, that the person has not yet committed any crime. Yellow means he has committed one, and red means several. Such a candidate would then be scrutinized even more closely.

I suspect you're feeling spooked. Isn't this the Orwellian surveillance state we're all so afraid of? You must first free yourself from the idea that you live in a state. The state monitors you only for one reason: it wants you to pay its predatory taxes. It justifies the monitoring differently, of course. For example, with regard to bank account queries it was said that it was about terrorism and money laundering.

In fact, the more than 350,000 account queries per year are almost exclusively about spying out tax slaves or transfer dependants. In the meantime, even the data protection officer paid by the state has noticed this. NTV reports:

By the middle of the year, almost the record level of the previous year had been reached. In 2016 there had been a total of 358,228 queries. As a result, 89,134 accounts were queried for tax purposes in the first half of the year, 69 percent more than in the previous year. The inquiries of the social authorities and bailiffs had even increased by 89 percent to 251,131.

This means that only five percent of inquiries do not relate to social affairs or taxes. How many queries have to do with terrorism, they don't say. Probably exactly one query, should Georg Bush or Barrack Obama have an account in Germany.

"Surveillance" in a PLS is of a completely different nature. Firstly, you agree voluntarily and only if the rule is of more use to you than it causes you anguish. No one has to take out insurance and no one is forced to carry an identification card. It is possible that there will be private cities or gated communities that will do without it completely. A gated community in particular can protect itself by guarding its external borders but allowing the greatest possible freedom inside. However, some kind of identification is necessary here as well, but this can be done by a fingerprint, for example.

However, I have strong doubts that people will have big problems carrying some card or device with them at all times. Most people today carry a mobile phone, on which all relevant data can be stored and which can also be used for payments.

And there I hear them again, the doubters, who think they're going to plant a chip in all of us. I say: never in a million years. Of course, there are already people today who actually do this voluntarily. But the mass of people won't do it. Maybe there will be gated communities for cyberfreaks, but I doubt that too. Of course, today there are a few brainwashed among the sheep who step up for such an experiment. But if there is no state, the constant propaganda also stops. Everyone is aware that freedom is a precious good. People only voluntarily renounce freedom when they consider it necessary to protect themselves. You don't need an implanted chip to do that.

I can guarantee you that I would be the first to start a company that guarantees its customers that they will never get a chip implanted. And millions of others would come up with the same idea. In the state, the chip will come anyway. It will simply force us all to do it.

Back to the data being collected: They serve only to determine whether someone is a professional criminal. It's in everyone's interest. Even a thief doesn't want to be robbed, only he can't do his "job" in such an environment. That brings us to what would happen to repeat offenders. Hans-Hermann Hoppe once put it this way in "Private Production of Defense", which I absolutely recommend:

Indeed, in cooperation with one another, insurers would want to expel known criminals not just from their immediate neighborhood, but from civilization altogether, into the wilderness or open frontier of the amazon jungle, the Sahara, or the polar regions.

But how exactly would that happen? Well, probably from the third offence onwards — here, too, detailed statistics would show when someone is to be regarded as an incorrigible criminal — one would make the criminal an offer that he cannot refuse. First, the penalty would be much higher than the first time. He would first have to serve the sentence and work through all the damages — with the incentives described above.

After that, a judge would give him a choice: Either he stays in prison forever or he agrees to be banished forever. But what's to stop him from coming back? He couldn't go back to the areas requiring identification anyway. He could also not rent an apartment, because tenants would of course always be checked anyway. In the case of a habitual criminal, however, one would presumably go further and require the planting of a chip, for example, so that it could be identified from a distance. Mind you, that's only for habitual criminals!

Of course, he could have the chip surgically removed. Then he still doesn't have an ID card. If he gets caught, they'd actually lock him up forever. He'd have to pay for it himself. As an alternative, he would be threatened with execution in this case. Such a regulation would probably be accepted by all righteous people. For who is planning to become a habitual criminal, to have a chip implanted, to have it surgically removed and to return to the scene of his crimes?

Of course, you can think up all kinds of lifeboat scenarios of an unlucky guy who is constantly persecuted by dark powers. It's stuff for science fiction novels. If you want to write one: Forget it! I'll do that. And if you want to beat me to it, at least name the hero after me. But seriously:

You have to compare these scenarios with the reality of today. Even today, innocent people are imprisoned and — at least in the USA – even executed. The likelihood that something like this will happen in a PLS is much lower, as each participant is constantly liable for his actions: the insurance company, the judge, the detective and so on. Who is responsible for false judgments today? NO ONE! Or have you ever heard that a state judge went to jail for a miscarriage of justice or lost his job or at least had to pay damages? Court companies that make obvious false judgments lose all their customers, the state doesn't and remains unchallenged.

It makes absolutely no sense to chase righteous citizens, neither economically, nor for reasons of crime prevention. Virtually nobody would agree, so it wouldn't happen. But it makes a lot of sense to get habitual offenders under control. Today, repeat offenders walk in and out of the courts, laughing at the victims and the police officers who arrested them.

Someone who relies on the state *not to* be chipped seems to be suffering from mental confusion. The state is the only entity that would really be interested in something like this and can enforce it with a monopoly on the use of force.

Even if you have a different opinion on individual points above: There is no doubt that the number of crimes would drastically decrease. Crimes against life and limb would be punished more severely. The world would be safer and fairer.

Corruption

A popular objection to the PLS is that rich people could buy themselves out of jail, for example by bribing a judge. That's a funny objection, because that's exactly the situation today. In a PLS it would be quite different, as you will see in a moment.

How could corruption be prevented in a PLS? Let us take as an example the one who would be most susceptible to corruption: the judge. You can, however, apply this to any position where someone is subject to a moral temptation (moral hazard) not to act in the interests of one's contractual partners, such as someone who has to decide on the payment of a reward.

First of all, it should be borne in mind that nothing would be more dangerous for a court company than to be given the reputation of employing corrupt judges. It would immediately lose all customers. The state, on the other hand, cannot lose any customers because everyone is forced to use its "services". This alone necessarily means that corruption *must* be more widespread in a state. *In* fact, this is the main problem in every state.

Some libertarians, for example, are surprised that even states that do not have a welfare state have low prosperity, even though the state does not collect a large part of the income of citizens. This is precisely because corruption is so widespread there that companies cannot be sure of their (fiat) property rights and therefore invest cautiously. This is the main problem (apart from IQ differences) in developing countries.

In general, the rule of thumb is that the more laws there are, the more corruption there is. First, laws are often the result of corruption. Large corporations dictate them to politicians in order to close off their markets through regulation, always of course on the grounds of "protecting the consumer". Secondly, laws originally invented by politicians or bureaucrats also increase corruption because they create an incentive to bribe those who, for example, decide on a permit or licence, or those who are supposed to enforce a law, for example a policeman.

So what could a court company do? It could agree on the following arrangement: When a judge receives a bribe offer, he may keep the bribe, but must report it. The briber in turn has to pay the money plus a hefty fine on top. It could also be agreed that the briber would automatically receive the maximum penalty for the crime he is accused of, and the judge would receive the same penalty.

Remember, all parties have agreed to the rules of the court company. Insurance companies would not accept other companies at all, as the scheme is entirely in their interest. Let's take an example: A super-rich man worth 100 million euros is accused of murder. He offers the judge ten million.

The judge now faces the choice of taking the ten million and remaining honest or pocketing the money and repealing the maximum penalty for murder. The millionaire, for example, could be deprived of his entire fortune and sentenced to the maximum penalty (possibly even the death penalty, because he himself has it in his hands to avoid it). In addition, he misses the chance of a mild verdict or of a revision in the next instance.

How much corruption do you think there will be left under these circumstances? Judges would also agree to their communications being monitored. That's just part of the job and compensated by their salary. They don't have to do the job. On the other hand, private companies would protect their judges much better than the state does today. Today, for example, you can often look up judges' addresses in the telephone book. Especially for judges working in the field of organised crime, for example, a PLS would contain quite different provisions.

Maybe they wouldn't even publish his real name. The judge would live in a specially secured gated community and be transported by armoured car. The state sometimes does the same today, for example in the mafia trials in Italy. But the judge still has to move through public space. In a PLS, the court proceedings could take place directly in the secured community, or the judge would only be connected via video conferencing. None of this is possible today or almost never the case. In a PLS, that would be routine.

Here, too, you must bear in mind the difference to the state: the state wants to force everyone to be monitored, in a PLS the judge voluntarily agrees to this. In a state it would be an absurd thing to keep the name of the judge secret, because the public naturally has a "right" to it. In a PLS, however, customers have a free choice. And victims of organised crime would probably prefer not to know the name of the judge when they see that these companies are better at fighting organised crime. As we will see, however, in a PLS organized crime practically disappears from the scene.

Again, perhaps my idea of fighting corruption is not the best or may even be completely wrong because of a mistake in my thinking. In a free market, however, thousands of entrepreneurs are working on the best solution. Since it is in the interest of every honest citizen to avoid this corruption, the best regulation will prevail. This is how real markets work. Also take a look at my other books.

You should deal with the so-called Truther issues because you will then realise that in a state, corruption starts at the top. The power elite wants a state because then they have to bribe, threaten, blackmail or reward only one person in order to cover up their crimes. That is why the power elite prefers very large units, the United States of Europe or preferably a world government. Then it will be sufficient to control just one government.

Here are a few examples for which you do not need to have any idea of investigative journalism:

Why is Angela Merkel not in prison when she violates Article 16a(2) of the Basic Law (Germany's Constitution) on mass immigration, according to which no one who enters via a safe third country is entitled to asylum ? This applies to almost 100% of all so-called "refugees", who are in reality illegal immigrants.

Why is the Federal Constitutional Court blessing the financial "rescue" of other countries, even though the Lisbon Treaty clearly included a no-bail-out clause?

Why is the Lisbon Treaty in force at all, even though it violates the Basic Law, because the people were not given a vote on it at all? Not only Karl-Albrecht Schachtschneider submitted a well justified complaint that this is unconstitutional. But even if one follows the argument that the people elected these politicians, one has to ask oneself why the citizens were not allowed to vote.

What does that even mean, elected? Even if the Federal Constitutional Court for once judges in the interest of the citizen and in 2012 determines that the voting system is unconstitutional, this has no consequences whatsoever. All laws passed illegally remain in force. Nobody's going to jail.

Worse still, the Constitutional Court demanded that the number of overhang seats be limited to 15. Following the 2017 federal elections, there are now a record 111 overhang seats! And they simply continue to govern!

The separation of powers is not only an illusion because everyone in the executive, judicial and legislative branches works for the state and is paid by it. Even if one of these state departments makes a correct decision, the other department simply does not implement the decision. The monopolist can do whatever he wants. So it's only him you have to bribe.

Now the topics for which you also need to know my other books and the research by alternative media:

Why doesn't Donald Trump arrest those within the Bush administration who carried out or allowed the September 11 attacks?

Why doesn't the Attorney General investigate the „Saxony swamp", although he has received thousands of files from the Department on Organized Crime (cf. "Die Vereinigten Staaten von Europa")?

In the NSU case, why hasn't the constitutional protection official Andreas Temme been arrested, who was demonstrably on the scene of one murder at the time of the crime and at least close to five others? The alleged NSU murderers could in no case be proven to have been on the scene. No description of the perpetrators that fits them, no DNA, nothing. The files are to be kept under lock and key for 120 years!

The answer is clear: Because decisions are made at the top and you only have to hold this top in your hand.

In a private law system you would have to bribe thousands of companies. Let me give you an example:

Let us assume that ten million euros have been set aside for the investigation of a murder. A detective agency finds out it was a gentleman named Anschelm Rockyfinger. Rockyfinger offers the agency 100 million euros and Sherlock Bribable accepts them. But that doesn't solve the problem. First, Sherlock has an incentive to resell this information and make extra money. Second, Sherlock would also face the same punishment for murder (see above). He may have 100 million euros, but he runs the risk of being caught for the rest of his life instead of being able to live in peace with the ten million. Thirdly, any other agency can also find the perpetrator. Then not just the killer, but also the detective would be caught.

Rockyfinger would have to bribe every detective agency. In addition, it's enough if the suspicious facts become public. Rockyfinger's opponent is now the company's well-funded insurance company, which pays the reward and receives part of it, for example, in the form of wages. Apart from the angry public and all the other agencies that are hunting him now.

All he needs today is to have Angela Merkel in his pocket. And he does.

Specialization

It is very important to understand that real markets tend to division of labor and specialization because it is more efficient and cost-effective. The judiciary is a very good example of this. Although there are certainly special departments and special chambers for economic crimes, the specialisation does not yet go far enough. Today, the same judge who decides on rape usually has to deal with burglaries and theft. Today, for example, police officers write their own incident reports. Like doctors, for example, they are constantly busy with bureaucratic matters. But a policeman who, for example, is good at keeping order on the streets because of his authority, may not be a wordsmith when it comes to writing good reports.

In an efficiently, i.e. cost-effectively organised detective agency, the linguistically gifted employees, for example women, would put on paper what their colleagues tell them about what's happening on the street. Here, too: It cannot be ruled out that in a police station today this will be similarly organized by a clever police chief. And it can also not be ruled out that a private detective agency is less well organized. In a market process, however, those companies that are more efficiently organized prevail over the course of time.

That's not the case with the state, which has the monopoly. All you have to do is look at any state enterprise. There are positive individual examples, but in a free market this is the rule because inefficient companies leave the competition.

Let's return to the example of rape. This is a crime fundamentally different from theft. The victims must be treated with a completely different level of sensitivity. Just listen to the thousands and thousands of cases of how rape victims are dealt with in the judiciary.

I can tell you a case that was related to me personally, but you will find such cases everywhere, so you don't have to believe me. A young woman was brutally raped by three foreigners of Arab appearance on her way home. The woman didn't tell anyone at first and called in sick. At some point she told her mother in tears what had happened, and her mother convinced her to go to the police.

There she was interrogated like a criminal. Just one example: She couldn't say exactly what language the perpetrators spoke. This is what the interrogating officer said: "Then how do you know they were Arabs? Are you a racist? " I'll spare you further details.

At some point she asked if she could talk to a psychologist because she was feeling so bad. The answer: "We don't have one, but we can have you sectioned." I swear it has been reported to me, and many other victims will be able to tell you similar stories. The upshot was: She didn't file a complaint, quit her job (because she doesn't dare to go to work anymore) and is receiving psychological treatment. The case does not appear in any crime statistics, but she now appears in the statistics for transfer recipients. The perpetrators are still free and may be raping the next victim right now. This is Merkel's Germany.

There are now enough mainstream reports about the acts of foreigners being played down and victims being advised not to report them. You will find links to current cases on my website. But even before mass immigration, rape victims were treated badly. The police is notoriously understaffed and inefficient as a monopolist.

In a PLS, specialized companies would of course take care of the victim. In any case, a woman would talk to the victim first. Psychological help would be right there, and so on. And why? Because that's what her insurance policy says, and she wouldn't have taken it out otherwise!

Of course, the courts too would deal with victims in a very different way: No humiliating public statements, no confrontation with the perpetrator. This is sometimes the case today, but only by the judge's grace. Just think of the WOMAN who acquitted the Turkish rapist! Unthinkable in a private law system. Today a public hearing is, so to speak, obligatory, which makes sense because the state often enough conceals crimes of the deep state. But in practice, filming is banned or journalists are handpicked when it comes to crimes that the state itself has obviously started. Think of the NSU case or countless others. The files of that case have just been locked away for 120 years! Why do you think that is?

Since this book is deliberately not written for Truthers and you may be one of those who believe everything that is written in the newspaper: I can't help you there. You yourself must come to the conclusion that you are being lied to from start to finish by the deep state, which includes the mass media. Please note my other works, books, articles and videos.

Back to the public hearing: This rule makes sense in a state that in principle cannot be trusted. But there are also cases where it is better to negotiate behind closed doors, but this is decided initially by the victim and not by the perpetrator. The perpetrator can still turn to the public with his story, if he was treated unfairly. Since this could mean the end for a private court company, they must be careful to judge fairly even behind closed doors. Whereas the state is always there, no matter what it does.

On the other hand, there are also false accusations by women. But even here, these really neutral court companies would be specialists. Because they have already seen a hundred other such cases. For example, it would be unthinkable in a PLS that a Jörg Kachelmann would have been remanded in custody, although it had long been clear that the alleged victim had sent herself the letter incriminating Kachelmann, the famous German meteorologist. Because the court enterprise — thus its insurance — is also held responsible if someone is wrongfully deprived of liberty.

Of course, misjudgments can never be completely avoided. But I hope you realize how in a market environment the number of errors would be minimized. The market is the most efficient system for detecting errors and finding solutions. It's not perfect, but it's light-years better than a monopolist. Anyone who denies this has had his brain wrongly wired, namely by the state education system. You may have a hunch why.

Specialization would also lead to meaningful rehabilitation. Once you have committed a minor crime, you will not be expelled from society immediately, but life is undoubtedly more difficult for you. This is precisely what creates the incentive to remain honest. But as I have already explained above, there is an economic interest in everyone being productive. This is precisely what certain companies could specialize in. They could specifically recruit first offenders, who would of course have to accept a lower salary. There would be no state that would prohibit this practice as "discriminatory".

The first-offender thus has the opportunity to get his slate clean again. If, for example, he proves himself for five years, he receives a corresponding certificate and can apply to normal companies. These would, of course, know his history. The "resocialisation company" exists due to the fact that it does as good a job as possible in getting someone back on the right track. It should make it particularly clear that its candidates have succeeded in doing so. Independent test companies could, for example, compile statistics on how people who come from these companies later prove themselves. Such test companies would, for example, be paid by insurance companies that adjust their tariffs according to the results.

It is not unlikely that first-offenders will become particularly involved, because they never want to get into such a situation again. Then their wages would be even higher. Or there is still a certain default rate and first offenders would have to accept a slightly lower wage. The decisive thing is this: The state constantly obscures what the true conditions are. For example, it does not raise the question of migration background or religious affiliation (more about this presently) with offenders. In a PLS, however, this data would be available and the companies could allow themselves to be guided by it. There would be no laws prohibiting the payment of lower wages to certain people. So there would be *real* market prices. This leads to more efficiency. Let me give you an example:

Maternity protection and the associated costs mean that women are less likely to be hired. The awarding of "social points" in dismissals means that people who start a family tend to be less in demand than young singles because they are easier to get rid of. The minimum wage ensures that people whose productivity is below the minimum wage do not find any jobs at all (cf. also „New World Order exposed": In a genuine market economy, everyone can live very well from his or her work, even if he or she has no qualifications at all) and so on.

By taking the state out of the game, even people who have made a mistake can successfully reintegrate themselves. Simply by adjusting their price to their reputation. The same then applies to loans. There will be agencies that lend money to people with worse track records at higher interest rates (which is forbidden today as "usurious interest"). If the debtor then pays back the money, his ranking improves again. Today he has to turn to dubious loan sharks, who cannot report a possibly successful debt settlement to the system (meaning today the Schufa) because their activity is illegal. The customer therefore remains in the clutches of the loan shark forever.

Another characteristic of specialization is that companies are usually successfully built by the very people who have the best knowledge of them. The reason can be experience, passion or special abilities. For example, a former first offender is most likely to build a successful rehabilitation company because he has the experience and passion to help others get out of their misery. The most successful rape court company is perhaps run by a former victim and so on. Of course, even in a state someone may have a personal interest in what he is doing, but there is no respective selection procedure.

If, for example, a police station takes special care of rape victims, perhaps because the police chief's wife has had such experiences, this will remain a regionally limited phenomenon. In a PLS, he could found a company that would take care of such cases worldwide. This is simply how markets work. Successful concepts spread incredibly rapidly worldwide because there is an economic interest in them. The state has no economic interest, because it can squeeze what it wants out of the citizens, and that is exactly what it does.

Specialization also means that a certain kind of people would get jobs who mostly do it for nothing today:

Job miracle for truthers

What's a so-called truther? A truther is someone who mistrusts official representations. He collects indications and evidence that contradict them. He puts up theories about what it could really have been like. Does that remind you of anything? It's classic detective work. Nowadays, detective agencies mainly work for cheated husbands and wives, because the state has a monopoly on real crimes. In a PLS, however, they would be the ones who would be constantly busy reviewing theories.

Let's take a particularly tough example: The truther who sits behind the computer all day, doesn't dare to go outside and has little contact with other people. Even he would have a place in a PLS, for example at the point where the detective agency checks whether it is even worthwhile to take on a case. This is first filtered out on the basis of the known facts.

This job can be done from anywhere in the world. The preliminary investigator can sit by the pool, with his arm around a beauty who loves famous detectives, or in a ski hut with a roaring fire and red wine. He can get up and go to bed whenever he wants. Why? There are no government regulations. The only thing that counts in a PLS is success. And if someone is particularly clever at combining facts, then the company doesn't care how and when he does it, the main thing is to keep to the deadlines.

The beauty is that even the more paranoid among the truthers would have their place. Some truthers tend to exaggerate pattern recognition. They sense a conspiracy behind everything, and nothing is a coincidence. The advantage of these people, however, is that they notice things that others overlook. Some might give the impression that they are on the autistic spectrum, who perceive too much at once.

In a PLS, however, these would be useful features that would be paid for. Today, truthers post videos on You-Tube that are either demonetized or deleted because they endanger the system. Hardly anyone of them makes money anyway. And the monopolist doesn't act on the information anyway. There are many truthers who have turned to the authorities with their findings, but of course nothing ever comes of it, because inevitably the state is always involved in these crimes, because it is the state that publishes the official version. The frustrating thing is that truthers can never prove their theories.

In a PLS things would be completely different. There would be a reward offered for solving the crime. The private detective agency is therefore interested in looking at the case from as many angles as possible. Let us assume that the truther found three striking contradictions in the files, which speak against the possibility of a natural death.

The truther reports these contradictions and also provides a theory. The detective agency thus calculates that it could be worthwhile to make resources available for the solving of the case. What would the chief detective do? He would rank the contradictions and start to investigate the most stark contradiction. So he would question witnesses in the real world, secure evidence, and so on.

If he succeeds in confirming the first contradiction, for example by exposing a false alibi, he continues. Whether a company commissions a truther or not doesn't depend on whether he can solve the case completely from the outset, but only on whether he discovers enough contradictions to make it worthwhile to investigate.

In today's world, the truther sticks to theorizing; he is also not necessarily the one best suited to really take to the streets and question witnesses or do other police work. And even if he were, he could never compete with the monopolist. Interestingly, left-wing or generally state-loving truthers would also have a place in the PLS. Of course, they won't tend to be as good at analysing, otherwise they wouldn't be left-wing or in love with the state.

In principle, however, political attitudes do not play a role in a PLS. There wouldn't be any politics. If someone is dissatisfied with his security service provider, he just chooses another. But he does not have to argue with others about the best form of government. He can only write blogs that don't interest anyone, because everyone else knows that all they have to do is change their service provider. But if this individual is still good at combining facts, he will also find a job.

I have also described this in a little more detail, because you can see that another kind of person would also benefit enormously from a PLS: The honest cop.

A paradise for honest police officers

The demand for honest police officers in a PLS would of course be enormously high, they would however have a different job title. What's the situation today? The police officer of today is overworked, badly paid and success is not rewarded. On the contrary, he has to watch the criminals he arrests walk free the next day. If he uncovers a major conspiracy in justice and politics, he is called off.

He may have had the dream of chasing real criminals. Instead he is used in demonstrations to protect the rulers from the people or the people from the antifa mob. He must allow himself to be spat on and laughed at, and if he takes a hard line, as at the 2017 G20 summit in Hamburg, then he will be investigated and not the antifa henchmen!

In a PLS, of course, there would be no room for antifa thugs. First, there would be no public places they could enter, because all places would be private property. Secondly, if they were able to cause a ruckus some-where, after the third offence at the latest they would be dropped by parachute over the Gobi desert or Siberia. Since antifa thugs are probably not suitable for productive work, the insurance company would prob-ably forego repayment of the costs, the main thing be-ing to get rid of the antisocial elements (see above).

Former police officers can thus take care of things which had actually drawn them to become police of-ficers: catching real criminals. They don't have to deal with harassing honest citizens who haven't done anyone any harm — think of victimless crimes. They would not have to take part in collecting the ransom that the state has imposed on every citizen: taxes are the state's ransom for not imprisoning you.

Even if someone didn't become a police officer out of passion, but only because of the money: he will earn more in a PLS, but he will also be paid according to performance.

Put it to the test: Give this book to a police officer you know personally. With that title, you'll have to do some persuading to get him to read it. Promise him a reward. You know, it's always about incentives.

The chances are not too bad that his eyes will at some point light up and he will immediately become an anarchist. He will know from his own experience that the situation for police officers is exactly as I describe it. And when he then understands that in a PLS he is automatically there to protect the citizens because they are his customers, he also understands that this is a much nicer job.

The first police officer who writes me that he has become an anarchist through this book receives a free copy, which he can then inconspicuously give to a colleague. But it must be someone who doesn't know me yet, because I already have several police officers among my readers who give me valuable hints that I use for my work. Of course, always under the assurance of complete confidentiality.

Of course, we all also know those public servants who cannot hide how much they enjoy having control over others: The psychopaths and sadists, who get off on exercising power over others. These naturally strive for such positions and are particularly frequently found in the judiciary. Research the incredible number of "scandalous judgments", "miscarriages of justice", "forced psychiatry" and so on.

Of course there is no room in a PLS for such people. As I have shown, the companies that will prevail will be those that pass fair judgments. They are subject to constant control by the insurance companies. If a judge or an employee of a security company acts particularly sadistically, he is dismissed more quickly than he can pull out a truncheon. A competing company simply cannot afford such people.

In the state, on the other hand, demand for psychopaths is particularly high. They must constantly enforce completely senseless laws, such as the persecution of people who have done nothing to anyone because there is no victim at all. They condemn "opinion criminals" although everyone learns at school, especially in law, that such a thing is the clearest sign of a dictatorship. You can only do that as a hardcore opportunist or as a psychopath. Neither is good.

In addition to this, another small excursion into libertarianism: As you see, in the private law system everything is permitted, as long as it harms nobody, because there is then no plaintiff at all. This is the golden rule and the basis of almost all ethical theories, religions and spiritual convictions.

Since virtually every law except those against fraud, theft and assault violates this rule, it means that judges are constantly imprisoning people who are actually acting in a morally unassailable way. This means that almost every judge today is acting immorally. Then one should not be surprised when the former judge Frank Fahsel comes to this conclusion in a letter to the Süddeutsche Zeitung of April 9, 2008:

"From 1973 to 2004 I was a judge at the Regional Court of Stuttgart and during this time I experienced unbelievable as well as innumerable violations of the law and perversions of the course of justice organized by the system, which can/could not be tackled, because they conform to the system. I have had to experience countless judges and prosecutors who can simply be called "criminals". But they were/are sacrosanct, because they acted on orders from above or were protected by the system, for the sake of reputation... It is not possible to take action against such colleagues in the justice system, because the system protects itself against exposure — through consistent manipulation. When I think back to my profession (I am retired), I am overcome by a deep disgust for my peers."

Since the state basically lives from robbery, there is negative selection at all levels in the choice of personnel, in a private law system it is exactly the opposite. Often the proverb quoted on this topic is this one: birds of a feather flock together. That's a nice saying, but the real reason here is that all the judges work for the monopolist.

In a private law system, however, competitors are very much interested in uncovering grievances on the part of their competitors. This is what companies do every day, in every industry, simply by presenting their product as the better one. As I have already shown, the court company itself has an interest in dismissing bad judges or preventing corruption.

If this cannot be clarified internally, it must turn to another court company, i.e. necessarily to a competitor. It has no interest whatsoever in protecting the competitor's judge. This in turn is to the advantage of all customers. But the state has no customers, even if it calls them that in the meantime, it only has subjects. That's why it gets away with such "business conduct."

The protection of children

A particularly important, but also tricky question is the protection of children in a PLS. In my opinion, this subject is far too often neglected in libertarian literature, so I will go into it in detail.

First of all, the problem is very clear: children are too young to claim their rights themselves. So who's going to protect them? We should first consider whether children are well protected in a state.

To start with, it must be said that the abuse, rape and even killing of children is protected from the very top. This can already be clearly proven by officially known scandals.

In the case of the so-called „Saxony swamp" it is about the child brothel "Jasmin". The official presentation on Wikipedia alone, which always feeds itself from mainstream sources, shows that this child molester ring is protected from the very top. Victims are prevented from giving the names of their clients. Journalists are silenced by libel charges. Involved are prosecutors, judges and police. The hands of the investigating authority, the Organized Crime Unit of the Saxon State Office for the Protection of the Constitution, were tied by the Saxon Constitutional Court.

Thereupon the department did the only right thing and handed the more than 15000 pages of files to the federal Attorney General. He refused to investigate. The Attorney General is bound by instructions to the Ministry of Justice and ultimately to the Chancellor. Particularly awkward: Thomas de Maizière, who was already responsible for the case in Saxony and who, according to research even by public TV channel ARD, covered up rather than throwing a light on it, was later responsible for the secret services, including the Office for the Protection of the Constitution, as federal Minister of the Interior. Minister of Justice was Heiko Maas of the SPD. Although the scandal in Saxony actually concerns the CDU, it is thus protected by the normally competing SPD party, and the other parties represented in the Bundestag didn't intervene either.

In the case of Marc Dutroux numerous witnesses died, the deaths were never explained. So it's quite obvious that the clues here lead right to the top, because Brussels is the seat of the EU Parliament.

During the so-called „Franklin-Cover-Up", which involved a child sex ring, the clues led directly to the White House and nothing has happened to this day. A jury found that the allegations were unfounded. But the Republican Senator John DeCamp always stuck to his presentation. You can check his evidence yourself and of course he has no motive to lie. He announced that he would add another book, but died in July 2017. Here, too, it is enough to have the monopolist on the use of force in one's hands.

In England it has now been confirmed that in the 1980s there was a child sex ring involving high-ranking politicians, police, judges, prosecutors, journalists and 261 celebrities. Most of the suspects are now dead. So they were protected for over 30 years. It is quite clear that these structures are still intact today because the names of the perpetrators remain secret. It's almost a miracle that anything has come out at all.

For decades the abuse of 1,400 (!) children in Rother-ham, England, by rapists of Pakistani origin was also covered up. The German "Zeit" even managed to conceal the origins of the perpetrators after the scandal was discovered, although every English newspaper wrote about it.

The former FBI chief of Los Angeles (Hollywood!), Ted Gunderson, reported about rapes and killings of children by Satanists in high politics, justice and media. None of this has been cleared up by the authorities. The mass media ignores his research worldwide.

But it goes even deeper. According to the statements of the psychologist and expert Dr. Andrea Christidis in the unmissable film "Maikäfer flieg",youth welfare officers took away hundreds of thousands of children from their parents — often on the basis of questionable expert opinions — and then often handed them over to the child porn mafia. Needless to say, she also suffers from constant attacks by the judiciary and is completely ignored by the mainstream. You can do your own research on the subject of youth welfare. A large number of parents on the net describe their powerlessness in the face of this authority.

In November 2016, a child molester's ring was discovered in Norway. The "Welt" writes about it:

Many of the suspects are highly educated, including lawyers and politicians.

Is it a coincidence that politics and justice are involved in all these crimes? This has to do not only with the fact that you have to be in control of the monopolist in order to do something like this, but also with the type of person that our legal system attracts. Rape means "taking innocence". In a state, judges constantly take away innocence from people who have not actually done anything to anyone, but have violated some arbitrary law. That's why judges already have the "mind set", i.e. the attitude that they may rob people of their innocence. So they're mental rapists to start with. Of course, most people are not aware of this and there are certainly a number of good judges. But it is clear from the outset that such a system attracts a disproportionate number of psychopaths.

The same applies, of course, to politicians. By definition, they think they have the right to rule over other people. Nobody has the right to rule over other people. But everyone has the right to offer his services on the market and to see if someone wants to use them voluntarily. In a PLS, psychopaths are firstly better screened out and secondly, neutral judges don't rob anyone of their innocence, because they always deal with people who have actually harmed someone.

It is also likely that women would play a much more important role in a private legal system, for example as mediators. Women are less interested in the exercise of power than in mediation. It might be more advantageous for insurance companies to send two counterparties to a mediator first. Since most disputants are men, it might be advantageous if a woman tries to mediate. The most successful mediators will prevail and I would bet that they will be mainly women.

I could go on forever here, but you can see the pattern. The cases that have come to light alone — also think of the Jeffrey Epstein case — involve thousands of children. The least that can be said is that the state obviously could not protect these children. But in reality, of course, it is clear that the perpetrators themselves are in politics, justice and the mass media.

But what would child protection look like in a PLS? Again, the principle of the neutral judge must be made clear. If the perpetrators are insured, the case is of course simple, they themselves have agreed not to abuse their children. But let us immediately construct the most difficult case of uninsured perpetrators who even abuse their own children to make it clear how it works.

First, it should be noted that abuse in the family is always difficult to detect, whether with or without the state. An outside person must notice something or the child turns to an outside person. This outsider is of course also insured in the event of emergency assistance (or hands the child over to an insured person if he is not insured himself and cannot or does not want to pay the costs himself). First, an example from the adult world.

Let's say you intervene in a rape and force the rapist to flee. Then nothing happens. The rapist could report this to some security company and charge you. As a rule, he won't do that, because then he practically turns himself in. If, however, the victim turns to her insurance and the offender is arrested, he has the cards stacked against him, because he would have to explain why he did not file a "charge". The case is investigated, the offender is convicted and he has to pay the costs. Of course, in a PLS it would always be clear that you can use every means at your disposal to ward off an attacker.

Transferred to a case of child abuse: Everyone would have the right to protect a child — for example from a single father who abuses it. For example, if the teacher, neighbor, shop assistant or mother of a friend notices something, she or he could question the child and immediately keep the child with her or him.

Then the father would have to sue for the return of the child. But with that he enters the legal system. If he is not insured, he could choose a court company from the portfolio of the helper's insurer. But he, of course, has to accept its rules, i.e. that he does not abuse children, and he has to assure that he would not have done so with his child either.

Is it to be feared now that in a PLS private citizens constantly take away children from their parents? No, because the insurance company is liable for the actions of its customers. It will therefore contractually regulate how the customer must proceed in such a case. He would then have to contact the insurance company, which would hand over the case to professionals. So either to a special department in the insurance company or to a respected child protection organisation audited by the insurance company.

In 2016, 14,000 cases of child abuse were recorded by the police in Germany. This offense therefore only accounts for 0.2 per cent of the 6.4 million crimes recorded. The true numbers will be higher, but you can already see the dimension. This is lost in the total costs, so insurance companies will certainly simply take over such cases.

An insurance company that, of all companies, does not protect children is unlikely to survive on the market. In addition, the insurance company should be assured of the child's gratitude and it would probably insure itself later also with this insurance company or even work for it, for example in the department for child abuse. I do not mean in this case the costs of the defense of the helper, the insurance company must bear these costs anyway.

But the question is what happens to the child now if a court decides that the child has actually been abused and cannot return to the father under any circumstances. For example, who will cover the costs of accommodation if there are no adoptive parents (such as the neighbours who helped the child) and have to go to a home?

First of all: Before the "refugee crisis", about 65,000 young people lived in homes, a sheltered flat or a shared flat. The annual donations in Germany amount to about five billion euros. That would be 76,000 euros per child. Today, however, the money mainly goes abroad for development aid projects. If there was no state, people would certainly first donate for local children. In addition, everyone would have three times the current net amount left. So one can expect that the number of donations would easily triple, or even more, because everyone knows that there is no state.

However, most likely the children would not be dependent on donations at all, because, of course, if abuse is found, the offender would still have to pay maintenance costs for the child, even if he is deprived of access to it. All possible sanctions, which I have already discussed above, are conceivable. Left over would be those children where the perpetrator evades responsibility, which should be much more difficult for him in a PLS.

This case could also be covered in any insurance policy, for example with a clause stating that in the case of child abuse discovered by the client, the insurance will provide for the best interests of the child. The insurance companies would simply offer this option as well. As we've seen, that would be a few cents a month. Probably this would even be part of every standard contract, because insurance companies would advertise that this case is automatically covered. Since really everyone, except for psychopaths and paedophiles, cares about the welfare of children, it would be hara-kiri not to offer something like this.

If the market doesn't offer something like this, you can simply set up your own insurance company to do so. You can be sure of success. You could book the additional few cents under advertising costs, because something like this would get around by word of mouth and be mentioned with praise by the media.

But doesn't that create a moral hazard problem in which parents would report abuse everywhere and even specifically go in search of abuse? No, because it's easy to prevent that. The clause could say that only one or two cases are covered. If there are more, the client would have to enter into a contract with professional agencies that specialize in taking care of such cases. This restricts the choice of cases to real chance finds, which, as shown, are very rare and therefore inexpensive to insure.

How could professional agencies finance themselves? Firstly through donations, secondly through commissions from insurers who do not want to offer this in-house, and thirdly through participation in damages.

As shown above, a perpetrator would have to pay for damages. Abused children often suffer all their lives. The corresponding claims for damages will therefore be high. The sooner someone becomes a victim of a crime, the higher the compensation, because he would have much more time to work without being affected by the consequences of the crime. An impairment therefore hits him much longer and the potentially lost income thus goes into the millions. For example, one third of the claims could go to the child protection organisation, just as lawyers in America already receive part of the awarded damages today.

It is therefore very likely that not only non-profit, but above all profit-oriented companies will take care of child protection. This is positive because these companies need to be particularly careful not to jeopardize their reputation and therefore their profits. They would be facing very tough competition, precisely because the subject is so sensitive.

In Germany, profit-sharing is prohibited. In a PLS, however, one would work almost exclusively with profit-sharing. This also guarantees that uninsured persons still get their rights when it comes to correspondingly high damage sums.

The commission need not even be deducted from the amount of damages. Courts could simply add such a value to the sentence. Let us remember: the jurisprudence would be designed in such a way that the number of such crimes is minimized. It is obvious that profit-sharing plays a role in this because it is by far the best way to achieve a goal. After all, there would be no state regulation as to which method or punishment is permissible and which is not.

Here, too, a considerable difference from the state can be seen: Child protection organisations as well as youth welfare offices, preschools or children's homes are extremely vulnerable to infiltration by pedophiles. However, a private child protection organisation would immediately lose all customers if scandals were to occur. The competitors would ensure out of self-interest the uncovering of grievances. So the security measures would be very strict and would include rules similar to those I described above on corruption. That means: Very high penalties for the perpetrators, high rewards for those who report abuse.

Since the perpetrators are almost exclusively male, I am also sure that those institutions will prevail where the work is done mainly by women. Again, there are no "anti-discrimination laws". And of course, no one would ever go to childcare whose holy scriptures worship a man who married a six-year-old and consummated the marriage when she was aged nine.

But wouldn't the efficient protection of children speak in favour of compulsory schooling, so that potential cases of abuse would be more likely to be exposed? Of course, one can always conceptualize extreme lifeboat scenarios of perpetrators who withdraw a child completely from social life and, for example, do not send them to a school.

On the one hand, even in a state, people who have evil in mind can withdraw as far as possible from social life. Secondly, I have already explained that someone who has no insurance has no one to defend him either, when worried people want to see what is going on in this lonely hut in the uninhabited forest.

Thirdly, one would need a state for compulsory schooling, which would include all the disadvantages of a state. Ultimately, by protecting children, you could also justify a totalitarian surveillance state in which the authorities carry out regular checks in every household. It should have become clear that children would be much better protected in a PLS, which does not mean that crime would be completely impossible. However, it would be much rarer and if discovered, it would be punished much more severely.

What about the legal age? Since there would be no legal requirements as to when someone has grown up, it is left to a neutral judge to make the appropriate decisions. Today, juvenile intensive offenders are judged very mildly. In a PLS, however, neutral judges would certainly come to the conclusion that someone who is able to churn out crimes by the dozen is adult enough to be punished. So the penalties would be higher than they are today.

Overall, the wishes of the children would be better taken into account in a PLS. So if a child says that he or she no longer wants to live with his or her parents, this would be more likely to be taken into account. There are numerous cases where the Youth Welfare Office has done nothing, although it was clear that the child was being abused, such as in the case of little Yuri, the girl Jessica or little Karolina. None of these survived. In the case of the girl Yagmur, who was beaten to death, the Youth Welfare Office even returned the child to the clutches of her parents, who had been classified as problematic by various authorities, after she had already been with a foster family.

I even remember reading about a case where the child had fled to the police for being abused. The police brought the child back and one day later it was found dead in front of the window of its parents' house. It would be unthinkable in a PLS that a child who turns to a private security company would be returned to the perpetrators. As already explained, private security companies are liable for their actions and insurance companies would certainly require that such a child be handed over to a child protection organisation.

On the other hand, the Youth Welfare Office takes children away from their parents for negligible reasons, sometimes even for political reasons. It can be enough to take the child to a "xenophobic demonstration". Even a "xenophobic" statement on Facebook can lead to child abduction. We know that the state already classifies it as "xenophobic" when ordinary citizens protest against uncontrolled mass immigration and the resulting increase in crimes against children. That would of course be completely unthinkable in a PLS.

Or take the incredible case Jo Conrad told me about in an interview. For years, the journalist has been providing information about child abuse by government agencies or high political circles. That apparently led to his downfall. A boy named Dave was abused in a state children's home and needed help. Conrad made contact with a woman who was willing to take the child in. The police showed up at her house and precisely the person who was responsible for putting the child into this home at the Youth Welfare Office took the child with them again! To this day nobody knows where the child is, not even the biological father! Jo Conrad and the woman who helped the child received a fine and a prison sentence from the court!

In a private law system, the biological father would have had to sue the helper (but he is obviously on the side of the helper) or a private children's home would have had to sue for surrender of the child. If it had then been proven that the child had been abused, the director of the children's home and other responsible persons would have been sent to prison and not the helper. If the helper had been insured in a PLS, however, her insurance would also have demanded that Dave come to a properly audited institution, or a neutral court would have decided whether the helper gets the adoption rights. In any case, the situation would be much better for the child.

If there are no legal requirements, when is sex prohibited with minors by today's standards? I'd like to turn briefly to the situation today. Epoch Times reports:

In France, Parliament will consider whether children aged 13 have already reached a minimum age for consensual sex and whether sexual intercourse under this age is per se and de jure forced, reports The Local.

Currently, the minimum age set by the law is 15 years. A case in Cape Verde, where in April a 22-year-old man had sex with an 11-year-old girl, is now causing a debate. The Frenchman was first sentenced for rape, but then only charged with sexual assault on a minor, as no evidence could be provided that the girl was forced to have sex.

One already suspects that this is connected with the Islamization of France, but one could certainly argue that the situation has been better so far. In addition one must know that with the state also the periods of limitation disappear. A child who later as an adult or at the age of 16, 17 or 18 or whenever comes to the conclusion that he or she has been abused by his or her father, for example, can sue at any time.

Of course, in such cases the gathering of evidence is extremely difficult, but that is also the case in a state. In a PLS, competing neutral judges would judge the case and not a judge who has to follow the prevailing ideology of the state. A neutral judge would decide alone according to whether the victim actually suffered or still suffers today.

As soon as a child can articulate his or her will, he or she will be heard. They can sue with the help of adults, such as a child protection organisation, and the organisation is awarded remuneration for its work by the judge if the allegations prove to be true.

Single mothers

What about single mothers in a PLS? First: If the incentive structure changes, people's behavior also changes. When women can no longer rely on the state, they become more cautious when choosing a partner. Extensive data is also available from the USA. When in the mid-sixties the US government decided to give more support to single mothers, their numbers exploded, especially among the black population. As a result, many children grew up without a positive father role model and crime rates in this population group rose as a result.

If there is no state, the behavior of women will change. Those who still want to live promiscuously would at least have their partner contractually assure them that they will take care of the children, if they become pregnant.

At the current state of technology, there would presumably be a "coitus app", by means of which both would commit themselves to certain conditions, such as financial support and the father's right to visit them. That sounds a bit unromantic now, but it's not much more unromantic than putting on a condom before having sex, which is what most people manage to do today without the world coming to an end.

But even if the woman is careless and the father lets her down, she has many more possibilities in a PLS than today. Everyone would have to work much less because taxes, levies and inflation were eliminated by the state-guaranteed money monopoly. Please note my other books and the works of the Austrian School of

Economics. Every woman can easily find a job in a PLS and earn enough money for herself and her child.

Abortion in a private law system

What about the protection of unborn life in a private legal system? Obviously, unborn children cannot sue. First of all, a look at the reality of today. Women abort, whether it is forbidden or not. In the Netherlands, for example, with its very liberal legislation, less than nine per thousand women have abortions, while there are many countries with much stricter legislation, where many times more women have abortions. In Africa, for example, where abortion is banned in almost all countries, 34 out of every thousand women have abortions.

It is undeniable that in countries and cultures where abortions are illegal, the complication rate is much higher, as abortions are often performed under unhygienic conditions and with questionable methods by mostly unqualified persons or by the women concerned themselves (self-abortion). According to the WHO, illegal abortions in countries where abortion is banned account for a significant proportion of the high mortality of women of childbearing age. Even if the figures are politically colored, common sense tells us that there is a tendency for more complications to arise if the practice is banned.

How would a private legal system deal with this problem? I personally now believe that abortion is immoral, but this is not about a moral judgment, but about what would probably happen in a private legal system. The woman must make her decision according to her conscience. Many women suffer their whole lives long from the decision to have an abortion. As stated above, in the absence of a state, people will pay more attention to the choice of their partner and, above all, conclude a contract before sex, strange as it may sound now. In this contract, therefore, the man could demand that his child be carried to full term and the mother would have to abide by it.

Without a contract, insurance companies would contractually regulate how to deal with abortion. Imagine the following case. A woman wants an abortion. The doctor discovers his conscience and delivers the child anyway. Although it is difficult to imagine that the woman would sue the doctor, an insurance company would like to avoid such a conflict from the outset. The insurance company would therefore write in the contracts that the woman should only have an abortion if either the child is incapable of surviving under any circumstances or if her own life is at risk.

Science says that babies are capable of surviving from around the 23rd week. Over 97 percent of abortions are performed by the 13th week and only about two percent between the 14th and 23rd week. So, to be on the safe side, insurance companies would probably demand abortions by the 13th week, because that covers the vast majority of cases anyway. After this period, abortions would only be required if the mother's life was in danger.

So, what would be the difference to the situation today? Today, organizations such as Planned Parenthood, which in its early days was funded by the Eugenics Society, are subsidized by the state. State schools and universities spread propaganda for abortion and against the family. Organizations like Pro Life, on the other hand, are privately funded.

In the USA, laws have already been passed which allow abortion up to the ninth month. One governor even went so far as to say that even after birth, the doctor and the mother still have the right to kill the child! The state is ever more obtrusively attempting to take the children away from their parents as early as possible and to put them in "day-care centers", which is demonstrably not good for the development of children.

At the same time, the state collects so many taxes and duties that it is becoming increasingly difficult to afford children. It can therefore be expected that a private law system would be much more child-friendly. There would be fewer abortions, but they would definitely be carried out by specialists. Doctors today also tend to diagnose a medical emergency, because that is the political Zeitgeist. In a private legal system, however, in case of doubt a neutral expert would decide whether the mother's life was really at risk, for example if the father sued, following the pattern of other court cases.

At the same time, a more affluent society tends to have fewer children, because in poor countries children are conceived so that one day they can feed their parents. Since in a private legal system all areas will be more prosperous, the number of children would automatically settle at a healthy level. The family would once again have a higher status.

There is no involuntary unemployment in a PLS

I have already dealt with this in detail in my other books and present the texts here again. But since the topic is so important, I will try a third approach to explain the matter to you. This is particularly important for basic income supporters who believe that technical progress will cause work to run out.

Productivity in Germany has increased about six-fold since the Bundesbank was established. If the basic income supporters were right, 83% of jobs would have had to be lost, as 17 people today produce as much as 100 in the past. In reality, people today would only have to work one sixth as much with the same standard of living. To make this clear to you, imagine the following situation:

Today, only about two percent of the population work in agriculture, compared to almost 100 percent in the past. This means that today one person can produce food for at least 50 people. So all you would have to do would be to appropriate unowned land or purchase some at a good price and feed yourself and 50 other people. If you cannot afford the requisite machines, then it would still be ten more people, but at least more than one. From this you can already see that there wouldn't be any unemployment at all, because you would only have to become a farmer and could feed yourself, your family and x other people.

But how do the others get the money to buy your food? Because they make something else that other people might need. Of course, it doesn't make sense to become a farmer if you can do something better or prefer to do something else. But no matter how much work the machines do in the future: Technical progress always means that everyone can afford more or could work less. Growth, which in reality is technical progress, is not a bad thing, but simply means that we can work less. In addition to these thoughts, read my other texts, whereby naturally the argumentation partly repeats itself. About growth I wrote in New World Order exposed:

The desert island: Is there a growth constraint?

Economists often use the image of the desert island to explain economic principles. That's a very good way of representing things vividly. At the same time, however, it must also be explained why the example can be generalized.

Using the example of the island, I will first clear up another big myth that drives many critics of capitalism. They claim that capitalism needs growth. They say this fixation on growth is a great evil and we should be more modest and also satisfied with less growth.

A colleague of mine at 'Focus Money' magazine once had the ungrateful task of explaining in an article why the economy actually had to grow. He couldn't find anyone to explain it to him conclusively. He then ended up with people who explained that growth was actually something bad. This is the school of thought of the Club of Rome. The only argument that the colleague then came across was that we needed growth because rationalisation meant that more and more jobs were lost, which had to be offset by growth.

In reality, we need growth in our state-monopolistic monetary system in order to be able to pay off the mountains of debt piling up in the state through compound interest — a race that can never be won. The simple truth is that the market economy needs no growth at all. It simply grows by itself, as we'll see in a moment.

So let's take a desert island with ten inhabitants. So far, they live off coconuts, which they pick. At some point someone gets tired of cracking coconuts and comes up with the idea that he could fish, too. At first he tries it in secret, because he doesn't want to embarrass himself. One day he proudly presents his catch to the others and lets them try it. The others find the fish delicious and offer their coconuts in exchange.

The fisherman can demand a relatively large amount in return, because he is the only one who knows how to catch fish. Since he cannot eat as many coconuts as he is offered, he demands other services. He allows his back to be scratched, air to be fanned on him or to be otherwise spoilt.

At some point someone gets tired of scratching the fisherman's back and finds out for himself how to catch fish. Due to the new competition the exchange value of the fish decreases. The easy life is over, but the first fisherman is still living well. Little by little the other inhabitants of the island decide either to fish or to crack coconuts. A new equilibrium is found.

Then someone discovers the ability to build huts and offers this service in exchange, and so it goes on and on. This market economy functions entirely without growth. Depending on their abilities and desires, everyone thinks about what they can offer and what they want in exchange.

Suddenly one of the fishermen has an ingenious idea, a technical innovation. Instead of catching each fish individually with his hand or spear, he makes nets out of bamboo ropes. With the loot of one single day, it can supply all inhabitants for one week. If there was a trade unionist on the island, there would be a lot of lamenting: That is unfair! All fishermen will be unemployed because of this nasty technology, we must ban that!

But our islanders are reasonable, and everything goes its natural way. Fish have become very cheap. The others can eat their fill for a fraction of their previous work. If the fisherman used his "market power" and offered the fish at too high a price, people would catch the fish themselves again, perhaps use nets themselves — or simply eat something else.

Meanwhile only one person offers coconuts, at top prices. Some go back into the coconut business, some exchange other services with each other. The high-tech fisherman has so much time that he could relax for the rest of the week. But our man has an entrepreneurial spirit. He develops a fast method for building huts.

Within a very short time, he has replaced the traditional hut builder, who then devotes himself to other activities. There are still ten people, they still have the same time available. However, due to advanced production methods, the inhabitants are suddenly provided with more goods. They have coconuts, more and more comfortable huts, fish and whatever else the inhabitants have come up with.

This means that the supply of goods increases and the quality improves without the population growing. The exchange ratios — prices — of the goods are constantly changing. The residents adjust to this, and the workforce is always directed to the areas where it is particularly in demand. But nobody is made unemployed. The most innovative can consider whether they want more free time or to invent more things. The less inventive look for an activity that corresponds to their abilities and for which they find buyers.

Even if in our modern society all goods were produced by machines, people would still not be unemployed. Someone would get too bored and have an idea how to please the others.

Supply creates demand, as mainstream economists say as well. Maybe the bored person will read poems to others or scratch their backs. In return, they would stroke his cheek or cut his hair. Work never runs out. It is distributed — without state intervention — simply according to the relative appreciation of the respective performance.

But is the example transferable onto a modern economy? It certainly is! The larger a society is, the better these mechanisms work. Ten people are still relatively easy to control centrally. One of them could, for example, become a chief. He then decides who fishes and who cracks coconuts. If he's a wise chief, he'll assign jobs to people according to their abilities.

But that's where the problems begin. Maybe the best fisherman doesn't feel like fishing at all. Or the chief doesn't like you and makes you a fisherman even though you are afraid of water. But even if he assigns everything as fairly as possible, there is no incentive to invent something. Because the chief will assign him a job anyway according to his, the chief's, taste. For example, when a fisherman invents a net, he depends on the goodwill of the chief to get free time in return. Tribes with such structures do not tend to progress.

It is precisely these structures — in communism or fascism and, to a lesser extent, in the social market economy — that hinder progress. If the economic subjects do not know whether their efforts will bring them a reward, because the state may punish them for their performance, then of course they also do less.

The island example is so well transferable because it is completely impossible to control millions of people. The wise chief would have trouble satisfying everyone with just ten people to deal with. On the other hand, the market economy with millions of people functions much better than with only ten. People can choose not only between coconut cracking and fishing, but between thousands of professions with different requirements.

One of the reasons why so many are still unhappy is our monetary system, which means that we have to work much more than would otherwise be necessary. What is important is that a market economy does not have to grow, but it does grow through technical progress. People's needs and abilities automatically balance each other out. Human labor is finite, inventiveness is not. That is why there are no limits to growth. But companies only have the opportunity to choose from the existing workforce. The prospering industries can pay higher wages. If trade unions in less sought-after sectors maintain high wages, this will only accelerate their decline. If the state then intervenes with subsidies, there will be no money to invest in new, more innovative industries.

Technological progress would make it possible for us to buy many more products for the same human performance, if the inflation induced by the state did not lead to a loss of purchasing power.

About unemployment I wrote in „Die Vereinigten Staaten von Europa":

Why there can be no unemployment in a free market economy

In discussions about libertarianism, one often hears the question as to where the jobs should come from, which must be available if everyone is to provide for themselves privately. A curious argument, because the free market economy is a job machine. Basically, it is quite simple: the labor market is a market like any other. Socialists then often object: People aren't products. They forget that labor is traded on every market. Every product you buy has been made by people.

On the market, supply and demand balance each other through the price mechanism. Most people actually learn that even in state schools. Everyone knows (or should know) the supply-demand curves. If the price is plotted on the Y axis and the quantity on the X axis, the supply curve runs from the bottom left to the top right: The higher the price, the more goods are offered. The demand curve runs from top left to bottom right: The lower the price, the more goods are in demand. The two curves intersect at the point where supply and demand balance. Although the market is never really in balance, it is striving to achieve this balance. It's the same on the job market. The lower the wage, the more work is in demand. The higher the wage, the more work is offered.

The latter is also the answer to the frequently asked question as to whether in a market economy evil companies can reduce wages at will. They can't, because then nobody would be willing to work. If things were different, there would be only one-euro jobs today, because companies are always interested in the lowest possible wages. But employees are interested in the highest possible wages and they meet where the entrepreneur still makes an adequate profit and the employee receives a satisfactory wage.

But that's all mere theory, the state disciple argues. In practice, evil entrepreneurs use their alleged market power and shamelessly exploit workers. Wrong. An entrepreneur must offer good working conditions out of self-interest, because otherwise the employees go to the competition. Today there are indeed some companies with poor working conditions. However, this is only and exclusively due to the fact that the state is destroying jobs through countless interventions — regulation and taxes. Every state intervention destroys jobs.

Any state intervention disrupts the price mechanism described above. Every regulation increases labour costs, so there is less demand for labour. It's a law of nature. It follows from man's nature to seek his own advantage. At the same time, people are also social beings who voluntarily show solidarity with other people.

There is therefore not a single state measure that creates net additional jobs. If, for example, the state subsidizes a certain industry, there is no money for products that people would have bought voluntarily. In a free market economy there is also no harmful "hoarding" of money (most likely not arbitrarily reproducible gold or not arbitrarily reproducible crypto currencies like Bitcoins). Since there are no government bonds, you can only increase your money if you invest it. (Even if people were to hoard gold out of risk aversion, that would be an advantage. Because this gold is out of circulation. The purchasing power of the remaining gold increases and the goods become cheaper, which increases the prosperity of all.) These investments create jobs.

Economists say that supply creates its own demand. Companies satisfy needs that most people didn't even know they had. For example, no one was aware that people would like to use cell phones without keys. Only one person knew: Steve Jobs. He just tried his idea and it was a hit. In this way, every single day, ideas are born somewhere in the world that attract investment and create jobs. Work never runs out.

How do we know? Apart from logic, the market mechanism can be admired wherever there are largely free markets: in supermarkets. The shelves are never empty. If the Socialists were right with their thesis of market failure, there would always be empty shelves or full warehouses. In fact, a little more is always produced than we need, because the companies compete with each other, but not all products can be sold. Therefore, there is always a latent shortage of labour in a free market economy. This is not a waste of resources because there is no more efficient system of resource allocation than the market economy.

In a planned economy, many more resources are wasted. The slight overproduction serves the purpose of trying out different ideas, because the entrepreneur cannot know beforehand which product will be well received. Overproduction is overcompensated by the fact that the best products prevail as a result.

Germany needed immigration in the 1950s because the then minister for economic affairs (or commerce secretary) Ludwig Erhard had introduced a relatively free market economy. Today, top performers are emigrating, hundreds of thousands every year. The "economic miracle" (only for socialists was it a miracle, for libertarians it was normal) in the fifties wasn't the result of rebuilding. The GDR had no comparable upswing, although East Germany was just as destroyed as West Germany. Millions of new jobs were also created in the USA, although they did not suffer war damage. This was simply because after the war President Harry Truman withdrew the job-destroying state interventions which were part of the "New Deal".

Over the next few years, all Western countries have become increasingly socialist and countless jobs have been destroyed. At 37.3 percent, the official state ratio in America in 2012 was only slightly lower than the German ratio of 44.9 percent — in contrast to the distorted picture that unsuspecting left-wing journalists paint of the USA.

But will technical progress not lead to job losses? Yes, but new ones are being created all the time. Productivity has increased more than six-fold since the war. If the state disciples were right, only one sixth of the jobs would still exist. But on the contrary, there are billions more jobs worldwide than at that time — taking population growth into account. This is due to the fact that in many parts of the world - especially in Asia and Eastern Europe –— the markets were left increasingly free, while in Europe they were strangled more and more. That is why jobs are created there and lost here.

Does globalisation not lead to wage dumping? In fact, globalisation means that certain products are produced more cheaply abroad. But we all benefit from that. The German worker can spend more of his wage in his country. In addition, German companies can buy cheap intermediate products abroad and "refine" them here through innovation and quality. The success of the German export industry at the time of the D-Mark, which was stronger than most other currencies, is proof of this.

Free trade always benefits both sides, as economist David Ricardo proved 200 years ago. The Ricardo effect also works on an individual level. The weak in particular benefit when everyone concentrates on what they do best in relation to their other abilities. That is even the case when they are worse at making anything than everyone else.

To explain the benefits of the division of labor, we go to a small island with two inhabitants, let's call them Strong and Weak. There are two ways to produce food, potato growing and fishing. Mr. Strong can do both better. It takes him five hours to produce potatoes for a day and four hours to catch fish for a day. Mr. Weak needs six hours for potatoes and ten hours for fishing, so in both cases he takes longer than Strong.

The division of labor, which only comes about through free contracts, uninfluenced by regulations, now means that both can concentrate on what they do best. Strong catches fish. Weak grows potatoes. If Weak were to catch fish himself now, it would take him ten hours. But he can also grow potatoes and trade them for the fish. So he only has to work six hours where it would have taken him ten hours before. The benefit for Strong is also there. He only has to work four hours for potatoes, where he would otherwise have needed five hours. Important: The weaker benefits more than the stronger. The strong person saves only one hour, while the weak one saves four hours.

To understand that we can never run out of work, imagine what you would let others do for you, if working hours didn't cost anything. They'd do dishes, paperwork, cleaning, driving, and so on. Craftsmanship would have a golden time again. Today, due to the high fees, a doctor has to work more than one hour in the clinic to be able to pay for a craftsman's hour of service. This is insanity. There is also a shortage of apprentices, because a left-wing press tells us that one is only worth anything if one has studied at university. Hundreds of thousands of people who are good with their hands are bored to death in office jobs. They then tinker at home in their hobby cellars instead of offering their talents on the market.

People who tell us everyone should study at university are arrogant, inhuman snobs. They're suggesting that someone is only worth something if he works intellectually. People have different abilities and that's a good thing. If everyone was as talented as I am with my hands, the country would be in ruins in no time at all. We must learn to appreciate it again when people have such abilities. Not everyone is an Einstein, but that doesn't mean they are worth one bit less. The "value" of a human being is not measured in money, but in his character.

Free entrepreneurs would also integrate disabled people much better than they are now under current law. Today, companies have to meet some quotas that generate costs, so offering many products is not worthwhile. How would that work in a free market economy? It's simple, a disabled person would offer his labour cheaper. Suppose he needs 10 percent longer than other employees for a particular task. He could, for example, demand 15 percent less pay. That protects him if the entrepreneur has to lay people off, because he is more likely to lay off the non-disabled first, because that is more advantageous for him.

But isn't this unfair and inhuman? On the contrary: the disabled person knows that he is not dependent on charity, but is paid according to performance. If public opinion were to strongly support this view, he would not feel inferior, but on the contrary a full member of society. Finally, he offers a benefit that is voluntarily accepted and decides for himself for what wage he will work, and where. The loss of salary can be compensated for by insurance policies taken out by the parents before birth. The contributions are minimal because the risk at birth is low. Most disabilities occur later, something no one can influence, and are therefore easily insurable.

Another point: In reality, disabled people are superheroes. If they lack a certain ability, they usually develop other abilities all the more strongly and surpass non-disabled people. Blind people, for example, usually have better hearing than sighted people. So they can do certain jobs better — for example on the phone — and then demand a higher salary for them. Of course, there are also people who are completely disabled, but as I said, you can insure for that. That is of course a small consolation, but no system in the world can rule it out.

The most important argument that you should always have at hand in discussions with state disciples: Even if jobs were scarce, there is nothing the state could do about it. If it finances unemployment or subsidises certain enterprises, it has to hand on the costs to the productive workers. Their work becomes more expensive and is therefore less in demand. Expenditure on unemployment rises, costs continue to rise and even more jobs disappear. There is no escape from this vicious circle — and we are already in the middle of it. However, this is due solely to the fact that the state has begun to impose punitive taxes, levies and regulatory costs on labor. That's what set the vicious circle in motion. We've got to finally understand this. Because lack of knowledge about human nature is the downfall of humankind.

The question of what to do with all the officials is also often asked. Quite simply, they work in the free economy and are paid according to performance. In a private law society more lawyers are needed, not less. There will be more "policemen", i.e. security forces, not fewer.

A good example is the relative liberalisation of the telecommunications market in Europe. The market is still highly regulated and UMTS licenses have created oligopolies, yet more people work in this field, the services are cheaper and better, simply because different needs are met.

The planned economy simply does not work because there are no market prices that signal shortages, as Friedrich August von Hayek pointed out using the example of East Germany. People had work, but it wasn't productive, which is why the state went bankrupt at some point. The planned economy is so unbelievably inefficient that it even fails when the state knows the needs of its citizens. Every East German politician knew that people wanted cars, and yet you had to wait ten years for the plastic bowl called Trabant. Can you imagine how much better a private justice and security system would be? We have a Trabbi justice system, but we could have a Mercedes justice system, which would be even cheaper because of the competition. The rich would pay a little more, for example for alarm systems, but they also have more money and a greater need for protection. The vast majority would pay less and receive a better service.

End of the book excerpts, back to the single mother: She could insure her children against disability before birth, which does not cost much because it is rare. She herself would only have to work a fraction of the time, so she would still be with her child most of the time. And she'd probably be more careful when choosing her next mate.

The protection of animals

What about animal protection: If you look at the websites of any animal protection association it will show you that animal protection in states obviously doesn't amount to much. On the contrary, pointless subsidies lead, for example, to animals being carted around under unspeakable conditions all over Europe, as reported in a Spiegel article from 2005. I doubt that much has really changed since then, but in any case the state has only created the problem it claims, in the meantime, to be fighting.

What would animal welfare look like in a PLS? First of all, it is of course absurd to place animals on the same legal footing as humans, something many animal rights activists are calling for, because animals cannot make declarations of intent. Besides, they'd be on trial for murder all the time. But people can make contracts and insist on their observance. For example, animal welfare groups could issue seals of approval that confirm gentle treatment of animals. They could be financed by the fact that these seals cost something. At the same time, the companies would contractually pledge to adhere to the standards of the animal welfare organization. If they don't, a hefty penalty is due.

There is a certain moral hazard that companies might set up their own animal welfare associations or bribe the organizations, but competing companies would denounce that. Today, most citizens rely on the state, which cannot be changed. However, an animal welfare organization that behaves in a corrupt way can be replaced immediately. One thing we should never forget with regard to this issue, as well as to child and consumer protection:

If there are no more politics, all that the press news sections could report on would be the protection of children, animals and consumers. The serious media would concentrate on this — in addition to entertainment — which leads us directly to the next topic.

Isn't this all too complicated?

You are probably a little dizzy from all the complicated mechanisms I am describing here. Isn't this all too much for the average consumer, who is obviously too stupid even to elect decent politicians? Doesn't a private legal order need rational, critical people, who don't seem to exist in abundance?

The good news is: No.

Here are two examples: Building a car or a computer is a complicated business. Most people have no idea how they work. But they see the result: a car that doesn't drive or a computer that can't calculate simply won't prevail. The core business of these companies is to build functional cars or computers. The core business of insurance and security companies, which would assume state functions, would be the drafting of contracts. The "moral hazard" problem, i.e. the fact that a contractor has the incentive to use information in its favor, would be the most urgent problem to solve. Therefore, the companies would put their focus on it.

Let us take a problem that I have not addressed so far: If someone dies and there's a suspicion it could have been murder: Wouldn't it be insanely inefficient if hundreds of detective agencies took care of it now and questioned all the witnesses umpteen times? Yes, it would be, and of course the professionals would be aware of that. This means that companies would come up with a solution.

For example, the company responsible for the payment of the reward could first have a certain company carry out a kind of general investigation. This is the only agency that initially interviews all relevant witnesses. Insurance customers would certainly agree to be available as witnesses within reasonable limits. It would probably be efficient to assure them of confidentiality for the time being. They are liable to the insurer for false testimony, so it would not be so decisive whether you know the witness. In order for the disbursing company to have an interest in the clarification, part of the reward could be offered to this company. That doesn't create a moral hazard problem, because a wrongly accused person could sue again.

In addition, rewards that anyone could claim would be offered for relevant information. Let us assume that the first agency does a bad job, for whatever reason. A competing company notices this and reports it to the disbursing company. This could now bring the obviously better working detective company on board, because it has a financial interest in solving the case. If a suspect is found, he is first questioned. If he flees, although he had the opportunity to express himself, he is put on a wanted list for all agencies and security companies to search.

What I mean to say is that it's difficult to predict exactly how the contracts will be designed in order to ensure effective prosecution. But one can predict that the contracts will be designed in such a way that crime will be tackled efficiently because insurers will have to pay less. Just as the tires of a car are round because otherwise they wouldn't roll, and computers use the binary system because otherwise they couldn't calculate. There's no need for a government order to accomplish that.

What about insurers who refuse to pay?

Today we often observe that insurers do not pay out at all. Mostly they refer to some clause in the fine print. Who would protect such customers who have themselves agreed to the scheme?

First of all, the current system is not comparable to a free market. There are numerous laws that create high hurdles for newcomers. In the insurance industry in particular, there are thousands of regulations that make it difficult for newcomers to enter the market. This leads to oligopolistic structures in which insurers can get away with more than they can in a truly free market. You can see this, for example, in the completely ridiculous opening hours of the banking oligopoly. On the other hand, the existence of a monopoly on the use of force also forces insurers to make their contracts more and more complicated.

For example, the general terms and conditions have to be adapted every time a state court judges in favor of a customer, even though he was actually in the wrong. Here is a real-life example. I once wanted to trade options at my bank by telephone, but had not signed the bank's risk declaration, which has to be renewed every few years.

When I pointed out that I have been writing professionally about derivatives for years and that I certainly could not sue the bank by invoking ignorance, this did not convince them. Why not? Because out of political opportunism state courts very often judge in favor of consumers even though they were in the wrong. This is why the banks' general terms and conditions are becoming more and more complicated and inscrutable. They're so long, nobody reads them anymore.

In the above example, customers who claimed that they had not been sufficiently informed about the risks repeatedly won their case. That is in most cases sheer nonsense. Anyone who expects a higher return knows that this entails higher risks. If customers then lose their money, some try to get it back with litigation. Since the state as a monopolist adjudicates arbitrarily, this increases the fundamental risk for any company. They react to it with ever more detailed general business terms.

It is certainly undisputed that people in a PLS would be particularly afraid of being exploited in contracts. But where there is a special fear, there is also a special need. You could, for example, as a company satisfy this demand for anxiety-free contracts. You could say:

Dear customer, I understand that you do not read complicated contracts and do not want to be taken for a ride. How about the following suggestion: Let me advise you — by telephone or in person — and we will record the conversation. You tell me exactly what you want and later we can present this tape to a neutral judge, who then decides whether you got exactly what you want.

In the case of health insurance, for example, the customer could say: "I want insurance that pays in any case, no matter what is wrong with me. I also don't want the insurance to be able to cancel, no matter what." That's very clear. If the consultant selects an insurance policy that does not cover this, he is liable. He, in turn, is insured with a re-insurance company which requires him to undergo appropriate training. In the market process, of course, it would emerge that insurers themselves offer this option. However, this also reduces the risk of the neutral consultant. He'd still be doing business with the particularly anxious clients. Of course, this has its price, but since there are no more taxes and levies, even the more anxious clients have enough small change left over for that.

Compare it again with the situation today. The state changes its mind about contracts as it sees fit. For example in Germany, it subsequently declares marriage contracts invalid because the partners are in a state of mental derangement if they were in love. The legislator calls this "emotional dependence". You would certainly not be able to uphold that argument in a PLS, but neutral judges would still check contracts for fraudulent deception. But surely private courts would not allow the argument that love makes people blind, nor that someone does not know that futures contracts are risky.

Today's divorce law has already financially annihilated countless fathers and unjustly deprived countless children of their fathers. Just talk to divorced people. It usually hits the better earner, which is sometimes the woman. But mostly it hits men, who never really get back on their feet. There are innumerable web pages on the net concerning this.

Could there be monopolies again?

By far the most common argument against a PLS is that new monopolies would emerge again. This is a strange argument, because the one who raises it acknowledges that a monopoly is bad. In the worst case this bad condition would be restored. But I want to use practical examples to explain to you that I consider it impossible for new monopolies to emerge in a fully developed PLS. Let's take a close look at the sector that would assume essential state functions in a PLS together with the security companies: the insurance market.

The insurance industry is one of the most regulated industries in the world. Insurance companies are even forced to buy up government bonds from the fiat money system, which means that they're in reality worthless. You can't just set up an insurance company. Countless requirements are demanded by the legislator. This means that the state has erected particularly high entry barriers here. So you would expect it to be particularly easy to build a monopoly here.

Are you familiar with Allianz insurance? Almost everyone knows it. Nevertheless, Allianz only has a market share of just under seventeen percent. How can that be, even though the market leader, in the opinion of the state supporters, would only have to buy up all its competitors? Well, that's not the way the market works. Let me give you an example:

Let's assume that a market participant from some industry already has a market share of 99%. It wants to drive the only remaining competitor out of the market by undercutting it. New entrants normally offer their customers an advantage, i.e. a lower price or better quality. But to make the case even more difficult for my reasoning, let's say both have the same production costs of 10 euros per unit in an industry with a total volume of one billion euros. The return on sales amounts to the usual average of five percent in Germany. Let's assume that the market leader is going five percent below its production costs to displace the newcomer. As the market leader, it must now satisfy all its customers at a cheaper price.

How long can it hold out? It previously earned 50 million every year and is now making a loss of 50 million. Its shareholders lose 100 million euros every year. The competitor, on the other hand, can lean back. It holds its price and only serves those who are convinced that quality is worth the price of ten euros. He could even buy up the market leader's product, which is cheaper than producing it himself. As soon as the market leader is broke, he takes over the entire business anyway.

Of course, rational shareholders wouldn't go through this for a year. The price of the share would plunge into a bottomless pit if a profit of 50 million suddenly turned into a loss of 50 million just to eliminate a small, puny competitor. This is precisely why market-leading companies hardly ever engage in ruinous price wars. And when they do, they usually go broke, too.

The market leader could of course also buy up the competitor, but then new ones will emerge. Everyone has the same good chance/risk ratio. In fact, there are many companies which are set up for the sole purpose of selling to a large company. There is even an extra expression for this in the venture capital industry: Trade Sale. This is not to the detriment of customers, as is often claimed. Because if the buyer does not implement the new technology, a competitor will. The market leader's customers therefore benefit if the company does everything right.

In a market economy, new companies are constantly emerging. Facebook has replaced MySpace (but not in a fair market process, more on this in a forthcoming book). Nokia sold the entire mobile phone industry to Microsoft in 2014 because it had missed the trend towards touchscreen mobile phones. Why didn't Nokia just buy out the competition if it was so easy for the market leader?

In a PLS, it must also be taken into consideration that there are no patents, so companies could not secure a head start by having any. They must constantly innovate in order to stay ahead. Any competitor could resort to new technologies as long as they cannot be kept secret, which is rarely the case. Today the state keeps thousands of patents secret, which can neither be bought nor used. These patents alone would have considerably increased people's prosperity.

In addition, customers always have different preferences. Even if there are no objective differences between products, some people prefer to drive a BMW and others a Mercedes. It is not possible for a company to address all target groups at the same time. Especially for the automotive industry it has been predicted countless times that there would be only one large corporation left in the end, because the investments would be so high that it would be cheaper, only one would produce all cars. The truth is that while investment costs are high, large companies are also less efficient. In every industry, new competitors are constantly coming in and doing something better than the old ones.

But what if one competitor fought the others by force? Now sit back and think about how you would actually do it.

Those who have the weapons are the security companies. So one of them would have to use force to take everyone else by surprise. But it wouldn't be insured. As I've shown before, there's no point in assuring anyone to rob everyone else. The security company would therefore be on its own and would be opposed by all the other companies and the large insurance groups. These would have the largest capital reserves because they would also have to pay in the event of major losses such as storm damage.

The insurance industry would therefore presumably operate globally, while security groups would tend to be organised on a regional basis. What's the evil security company, let's call it Darth, supposed to do now? Firstly, it would have to make its preparations secretly, as certainly none of the customers would be prepared to co-finance an attack on all the others. After all, they want protection against attacks and not to pay double the price for their neighbours being attacked.

But suppose some rich psychopath manages to set up a secret army? Where does he start now? He could occupy the headquarters of a competitor. Then what? It's just the administration. The security guards are distributed among their customers. Would they now pay Darth just because he's occupied the headquarters? Of course not. So Darth would have to go to every single customer every month and squeeze the money out of them, that is, fight thousands of small battles against all the other security companies. It would have to be clever enough to outwit thousands of companies that own the streets and the gated communities. They'd have to disguise their tanks as ice-cream vans to even be able to use a road.

He probably wouldn't get any staff for a crazy plan like that. But even if he initially conceals the plan from them, at some point he would have to say what it is all about. So the employees would have the choice of warning a competitor (for a reward of course) and working there or of getting involved in such a suicide mission — with all security companies, all insurance companies with huge capital reserves and all ordinary citizens against them.

Even if the psychopath had managed to win 50% of the market with previously honest work for the client, as soon as he revealed his true plan, he would lose all his clients and probably most of his employees in one fell swoop. Up until now the employees had a good job. Now and then catching a criminal and permanently waging war are two completely different things.

Then why are there any wars at all? Well, because the state works completely differently. First, the citizens are forced to finance its adventures. But that's not even the most important thing. The state doesn't really exist. It is only a particularly stubborn illusion maintained by the high priests of the state, the "intellectuals", i.e. the liars trained by the state. There are less than 300,000 police officers in Germany. If people stopped paying taxes overnight, they would never be able to be collected. People only pay because they think they have to pay for services they haven't asked for.

But in a PLS there wouldn't be anyone else except a few crackpots who would believe in such an absurd concept. Not only would private schools naturally explain to children that no one has the right to rule over others, or that the judge must not be part of the conflict. A five-year-old who cries out for his parents when he comes into conflict with his brother or buddy understands that.

It is mainly the daily experience that would make people lose this superstition that they have to pay for services that they haven't asked for. So even if someone were to get nuclear weapons and threaten everyone with them, everyone would know he was the bad guy. No one would object if he was simply eliminated. More about that presently.

What would happen if the largest companies merged to form a state? Well, then all customers would go to a smaller or completely new competitor. Most of the employees of the former market leaders would also be gone immediately, because they would be equally enslaved. Until that point, they were automatically protected — practically free of charge — by their own security company and its insurance company. They could choose their employer and working conditions.

After the establishment of a state, they would have to pay part of their income as taxes themselves and, of course, they would suddenly have to pay the taxes of the companies and their employees when purchasing their goods. So far, they've protected their customers. Now they would have to monitor, harass and hassle their former customers for the monopolist for victimless "crimes" and for them to pay their taxes for services they did not ask for. And this despite the fact that the security staff themselves experienced that there are other ways.

Do you seriously believe that anyone who has ever experienced a PLS would suddenly accept that from now on his rates are to be unilaterally determined by the monopolist, after years of deciding for himself how much to pay whom?

That's a completely crazy idea that you can only come up with when you've grown up in a state. Or would you accept that as of tomorrow all car manufacturers would join forces and force you to buy cars for 70% of your salary?

Defense in a private law system

It should now be clear that it is virtually impossible to reinstall a state in a private law system. Crimes would be regional phenomena that would be fought on the ground. Weapons of mass destruction would be totally unsuitable and therefore far too expensive. But since states like to wage war, they still have weapons of mass destruction. How would private security companies react?

It is important to understand that states are, of course, very inefficient on this issue too. They live on stolen money and therefore procure weapons that in reality are useless. The money is bagged by the military-industrial complex. It is almost impossible to conquer the territory of a private law system, since citizens would potentially be armed. The USA can't even conquer Afghanistan permanently, and those people fight with slingshots, so to speak, against the world's largest military power. There would certainly be gated communities in which, for example, everyone would agree not to carry weapons, but these would then be protected by armed professionals. A state opponent therefore will encounter either professionals or armed ordinary citizens.

Private insurance companies would also require their customers not to commit crimes in states, for example to trade drugs, because this could be used by states as an excuse to invade. People like that would be handed over. People who do not insure themselves and trade drugs in a state would be extradited anyway. Nobody's protecting them.

So there would be no plausible reason for other states to attack a PLS. Known public servants would certainly not have access to a PLS either. Private insurance companies would rule out insuring someone who invites such people into their homes. They would rightly be considered terrorists.

But let's just assume that by clever propaganda a state has managed to get its population to support it. Private security companies would then focus on the actual aggressor, not on the population, which would be seen as potential customers. So they would tell the leader of the aggressive nation through secret channels that they would kill him if he prepared a war of aggression. That would of course be morally justifiable just as much as shooting someone who with a weapon threatens to rape a woman, however the moral question is not raised here at all, but the economic question instead. The turnover of the private security companies is ultimately in danger.

They could make the following offer to the leader of the neighboring nation:

1. You can change your state into a PLS and get a well-endowed supervisory board position in one of our companies.
2. You keep that up, and we'll do you in.
3. You do not turn your state into a PLS, but you remain peaceful and can at least continue to exploit your own subjects.

What would you choose? Let's assume the first one dismisses the warnings. They'd eliminate him, but not in a way that's obvious. He would simply die, just as people who have become too dangerous for the system die prematurely today. Remember, private companies would be extremely efficient. If the CIA can just take people out, a private security company certainly can. But it would not, as in a PLS, have the security companies of innocent citizens against itself.

One would also explain to the next leader in a coded way that his predecessor was eliminated. How many leaders do you think you'd have to kill before one of them decided not to march in?

You should recognize that even today there are already numerous states that are organized almost like a private law system, have very low taxes and have not yet been invaded. Examples would be the Principalities of Liechtenstein and Monaco. You need a good reason to convince your people to attack an innocent neighborhood. Probably even people close to the respective leader of the country would eliminate an aggressive president. At the very latest, when the latter hides in a bunker and the private security companies start to eliminate those circles around the president who are not sitting in the bunker.

You must always bear in mind that this is the most economically sensible approach. Once you understand this, you also understand that most wars are set in motion by forces acting on both sides. For example, if you take a closer look at German history and disregard the official fairy tale books, you will find that Hitler could have been killed much sooner.

But the German resistance was betrayed again and again by the Allies. Simply because this war was desired by the influential circles and Hitler provided the perfect demon to convince the world public of the need for war. In reality it was mainly about the destruction of Germany as a competitor on the world markets, but that is a subject for another book. In the case of Saddam Hussein and Muammar al-Gaddafi, they wanted these two dead, and, lo and behold, they made it happen.

What had finally been destroyed in Germany was the military and the people's belief in themselves, but not their belief in the state. It was even extended and so a puppet regime could be established, which led the people to believe that it was there for them. In a PLS, however, there is no longer any belief in domination, but only trust in the best voluntarily paid service provider.

Immigration without borders

Immigration is the biggest security risk today. However, this was already the case before the refugee crisis. According to official statistics, foreigners are on average three times as criminal as German passport holders. However, this is due to the fact that harmless offenses such as environmental crimes are also covered. In the relevant crimes such as murder and manslaughter, dangerous and serious bodily injury, rape and sexual assault, theft in aggravating circumstances and predatory attacks on drivers, foreigners are four times more criminal than their proportion of the population.

However, the statistics don't include the migration background. Studies show that second-generation immigrants are even more criminal than their parents. A cautious assumption would therefore be that people with a migration background are just as criminal as their parents. Then the following picture emerges. One in five Germans now has a migration background. Every tenth is a foreigner. Rule of three: Out of every 100 people, 20 with a migration background commit four crimes each, ten foreigners four each and 70 ethnic Germans one each. This means that foreigners and those with a migration background already commit almost two thirds (63%) of the crimes. Since second generation immigrants are more criminal, the number is likely to be even higher.

The former Berlin Senator of the Interior Thilo Sarrazin has put on record that 80 percent of the food distribution in Berlin's juvenile prison is now halal, i.e. Muslim. Since not all Muslims are strict believers and not all foreigners are Muslims, more than 80 percent of the inmates must have a migration background. Now you could claim that Sarrazin exaggerates, because he is known to be an immigration critic.

But sources that are above suspicion in this regard confirm this picture. On 18 November 2013, the German news journal 'Focus' quoted the Berlin senior public prosecutor as saying this:

80 percent of Berlin's repeat offenders have a migration background. Most of them — 43 percent — are of Arab origin, 32 percent come from Turkey.

These are Muslim countries, so Sarrazin's statement is probably correct. In most European countries the migration background is not recorded, but other statements from the judicial system paint a similar picture.

On 29 May 2017, "Focus" informed us that the Minister of Justice of the state of Hesse was worried because fewer and fewer prison inmates were speaking German:

According to state Justice Minister Eva Kühne-Hörmann (CDU), every second prisoner in Hesse speaks insufficient German. According to the "Bild" newspaper, this figure is as high as 75 percent in Wiesbaden Prison.

If you assume that there are also criminals with a migration background who speak German, you can roughly imagine what's going on.

The situation is similar in neighbouring Austria: This is what the English Express wrote on 9 December 2016:

A member of law enforcement in Vienna's largest judicial institution, who did not want be named, said:

"The number of 'real' Austrians [convicted] for rapes is negligible. There are big problems with other cultures." There are similar findings in Sweden. The Gatestone Institute reports on February 14, 2015:

In 1975, the Swedish Parliament unanimously decided to transform what had previously been a homogenous Sweden into a multicultural country. 40 years later, the dramatic consequences of this experiment become apparent: the number of violent crimes has risen by 300 percent. If you look at the number of rapes, the increase is even more serious. In 1975, 421 rapes were reported to the police, in 2014 there were 6,620, an increase of 1,472 percent.

Sweden now ranks second in the world in terms of the number of rapes in relation to the size of the population. According to a 2010 study, Sweden, with 53.2 rapes per 100,000 inhabitants, is only surpassed by tiny Lesotho in southern Africa with 91.6 rapes per 100,000 inhabitants ...

Since 2000 there has been only one study on immigrant crime in Sweden. It was conducted in 2006 by Ann-Christine Hjelm from the University of Karlstad. It turned out that in 2002, 85 per cent of those sentenced to at least two years in prison for rape by the Svea Hovrätt, a court of appeal, were born abroad or second-generation immigrants.

A 1996 Swedish National Council report on crime prevention concluded that immigrants from North Africa

(Algeria, Libya, Morocco and Tunisia) were 23 times more likely than Swedish men to commit rape. The figures for men from Iraq, Bulgaria and Romania were 20, 18 and 18. Men from the rest of Africa were 16 times more likely to rape, men from Iran, Peru, Ecuador and Bolivia ten times more than men from Sweden.

In Oslo, Norway, the rate of rapes committed by perpetrators with a migration background between 2006 and 2010 was, according to a 2011 study, 100 percent!

These are all figures from before the "immigration crisis". The so-called "refugees" are even more criminal. Although it was not reported in a single mainstream medium, the BKA report shows that in 2016 asylum seekers were fifteen times, i.e. 1,400 percent, more criminal than German passport holders with regard to violent acts and sexual crimes and even 42.6 times more criminal with regard to gang rape. If the comparison was only with Germans without a migration background, the figures would be much higher. But even a factor of 15 means that if there were an equal distribution between asylum seekers and people with a German passport, 93.4 percent of all violent crimes would be committed by asylum seekers!

Patriots in particular often raise the objection that, without a state, a community can't protect itself from dangerous immigration. Nothing could be more wrong. First of all, let's investigate immigration from a logical-libertarian point of view. I use this word because there are indeed people who call themselves libertarian who at the same time are in favour of open borders. These are the so-called Liberalalas, false libertarians or "Stupids for Liberty", as Hans-Hermann Hoppe once put it wittily. Libertarian is not a protected term. Anyone can call themselves that, even if they have no idea of logic.

Open borders for goods and open borders for people are mutually exclusive. Free trade is based on the voluntary contract between two people. To prevent this is a restriction of property rights, which comes about through the fact that the monopolist on the use of force, as the ultimate judge, presumes to decide for himself what is good for his subjects.

Uncontrolled mass immigration is also a restriction of the property rights of its citizens. In a PLS, someone can only enter the property of its residents if someone invited them. In a state, however, the roads are public, primarily because the state wants free access to its subjects in order to collect taxes.

The subject is thus restricted in his property rights in several ways: firstly, he does not have the opportunity to keep criminal subjects away from him because he also has to use the public roads. Secondly, he has to pay taxes for the prosecution of these criminal subjects. Thirdly - and particularly devastating in a welfare state like Germany - he must also pay the transfer payments for the uninvited "guests".

So the solution in a state can only be to only let in people who have an invitation. This can be pronounced by a company that wants to recruit employees, by tourism companies that want to do business, by landlords and sellers of houses or by private aid organisations. Of course, the inviting party would have to be liable for the guests, which leads to them looking closely at who is coming in. The use of the welfare state would of course also be impossible.

How much of the problematic migration would we still have then? Pretty much zero.

Immigration without invitation by a specific person is always forced migration, thus the exact opposite of a voluntary transaction. Free trade and free migration are therefore mutually exclusive.

This also makes it clear how this would work in a PLS: There would be no mass migration of parasites and criminals, the only people who would come are those who were invited by someone. Private security companies would also have very accurate data on how dangerous a particular population group is on average. These would be considered with particular suspicion, but more about that presently.

So what would the territory of today's Germany look like if it had been transformed into a private law system after the war? Much more German than today. But not necessarily in an ethnic sense. A PLS would of course attract productive people from all over the world. However, if there were a PLS worldwide, there would be no reason to migrate, because the conditions would be better everywhere. Most people would like to stay in their home country if the conditions there are good.

In a PLS, there would be no laws against discrimination, so companies could also decide to hire only ethnic Germans, but it would be highly unlikely that this would happen on a massive scale. But the area would be much more German in a cultural sense. Criminals would have little chance because they would be pursued more effectively and would probably be parachuted over the Gobi Desert at the latest after the third minor offence or would be locked away forever in the event of more serious offences.

Only people who are productive and who help society in this way would come. These would have values such as punctuality, diligence, reliability, honesty, quality awareness, organisational skills, love of order, inventiveness and the like, i.e. precisely those values that could be described as typically German. Only one quality, which is also ascribed to the Germans, would be missing: Subservience to authority. Since the authorities are missing, this unpleasant characteristic of the Germans would be eradicated in one go.

I believe, however, that subservience to the authorities is owed to two other qualities of the Germans: love of order and honesty. Honesty tempts the Germans to believe everything the ruling class says. It can be proven experimentally that people assume in the other the qualities they have themselves (projection theory). This is also a big problem with regard to the so-called refugee crisis. The Germans cannot imagine that there are cultures with a much higher degree of violence and contempt for women, although this is statistically easy to prove. Germans are thus not so much subservient to authority, as believers in authority. There were also repeatedly freedom struggles in Germany when even the Germans realized the lies of the rulers.

Because of their belief in authority, Germans also think that they owe the relatively good order in Germany to the state. They love order, so they love the state. A glance at almost all other countries would be enough to see that nothing there is as orderly as in Germany. However, thanks to mass immigration, Balkanization has long since begun in Germany as well. In reality it is (was) so orderly in Germany, because the people there are (were) orderly. Germans could therefore be the fastest to implement a private law system, and it would be the best working one. I am also quite sure that in a worldwide PLS German insurers and security companies would quickly become leaders.

This is all the more true since there would also be free historical research in a PLS and the truth about German history would come to light. Then the German way of life would actually heal the world, but not through coercion and conquest, but through performance and example.

By the way, in such a world there would be borders. As long as there is no worldwide private law system, the other states would not only guard their borders, but probably very quickly raise walls because they would be quickly losing their most productive citizens. That was also the reaction of the GDR, but even these walls fell at some point, however not yet in favor of a truly libertarian order, because such an order did not yet exist.

What the path to a private law system could look like is the subject of another book. But this much can already be revealed at this point: We are already in the middle of an evolutionary process toward it. New technologies such as "blockchains" can already authenticate property rights and contracts in a decentralized way.

Private cities or gated communities today already fulfil almost all tasks that are still regarded as "public" (today). There are roads, hospitals, fire brigades, lakes, nature, playschools, private security and so on. Needless to say, without exception, crime rates there are much lower than in the areas around them. The residents would only have to agree to turn to a neutral judge in conflicts, and the private law system would already be perfect. In my emigrant project Project Escape, a corresponding clause is already included in the contracts.

The inhabitants of these cities will soon wonder what they are still paying taxes for, especially when the state is becoming more and more repressive.

On immigration, please also note the works of Hans-Hermann Hoppe: "The Great Fiction", "The Case for Free Trade and Restricted Immigration" and "Natural Order, the State, and the Immigration Problem".

The end of no-go-areas

It should by now have become clear that crime rates in a PLS are falling drastically. However, we now want to deal with a particularly difficult case in order to make it clear how the civilizing process actually takes place. Let us assume that an area such as Germany, Sweden or France were to be converted into a PLS. Areas that are already no-go areas today would of course react differently from areas that have a low crime rate anyway.

The insurance companies would offer individual insurance rates for each region. In areas with high crime rates, the insurance rate would be higher. Don't forget that at least everyone who works has immediately much more money available. In civilized areas, the price of security today would slide from 80 to 25 euros or less, as explained above. But in the bad areas too the price would be much lower than a worker pays today in taxes and levies.

Here is a brief numerical example from my book „Die Vereinigten Staaten von Europa":

100,000 people live in the Schwabing district of Munich, which is quite clearly laid out. If each of them spent 10 euros a month on a security company, one million euros a month would be available. If the security guards were paid a salary of 2500 euros for a job for which they do not need to study and which they would get gross for net, 400 security guards could be employed to patrol alternately around the clock.

Today in Schwabing, where I live, you hardly ever see a policeman unless he issues parking tickets instead of chasing criminals. That's a multiple of what's being done today for your safety. So you can double the salary or halve the number of cops. If then you add to each "policeman" another "justice employee", thus a lawyer or arbitrator, which is a much too pessimistic estimate, you are still paying only 10 euros. It's nothing. You can see from this how incredibly inefficient the state is. Our judiciary is not concerned predominantly with the protection of citizens, but with their persecution and surveillance.

Even if 800, 1,600 or 3,200 security guards were needed in a no-go area, we would still easily remain below 100 euros per citizen. But back to insurance: Even in a no-go area, most people are not criminals. They allow themselves to be terrorized by a minority because the state is not doing its job properly. As we will see in the chapter on the mafia, this is also due to the fact that it infiltrates the state and bribes judges, police, politicians and judicial employees.

In our case, however, the criminals are dealing with huge insurance companies for which a single no-go area represents a balance sheet item that is not even noticeable.

First of all, insurance companies would compile precise statistics on the actual structure of the area: it would record the number of migrants, their nationality or migration background, their religion and skin colour, and so on. The state is hiding this data today for political reasons. The insurance company would say to the owner of a house, for example, that the premium would be drastically reduced if he kicked out all members of a high-risk group. The owner would probably do this inconspicuously if he didn't want to cause trouble immediately. This alone sets off a process of civilization. Members of a risk group would also have to pay higher premiums, just as young male beginner drivers had to pay higher premiums in the past.

But the state has also intervened in the meantime with regard to insurance premiums. The European Court of Justice has banned gender-specific contracts, despite the fact that women are now causing fewer accidents and living longer. For men, for example, this means that Riester contracts (grant-aided privately funded pension scheme in Germany) become unattractive. It is grotesque. But just as the premium for a beginner driver decreases if he proves himself, so the premium for someone who belongs to a high-risk group in terms of crime but remains blameless would decrease.

Although discrimination is not "prohibited" in a PLS, insurance would be blind to ideologies in a certain way. For example, if those who claim that Islam is such a peaceful religion were right, the premiums for Muslims would be even lower. So if you ever talk to an Islamic apologist, you could use this argument to make a PLS palatable to him.

But then you shouldn't tell him that no insurance company in the world would accept the rules of Sharia law. Women there, for example, are worth only half as witnesses. Since half of the customers are female, this rule would certainly not be offered, not to mention many others. Islam also expressly contains a mission of conquest. Please read the book "The Story of Mohammed – Islam Unveiled" by Harry Richardson. It refers exclusively to official sources from the holy scriptures of Islam.

In the Koran there are several explicit calls to kill infidels. It is even recommended in the Scriptures to make covenants with unbelievers in pretence, to gain their trust and then kill them. Deception is explicitly proposed as a means of conquest. This is completely concealed by our state universities and mass media, but a private security company would of course know that. You must remember that all Muslims are called to learn the holy scriptures of by heart. So those who have done so know of the scheme, but have Muslims ever told you about it?

Of course, most Muslims are not so radical, but the risk is considerably higher than with someone who does not carry such instructions in their luggage or even has to learn them off by heart. Private companies would probably only insure a Muslim if he voluntarily agreed to such monitoring and, of course, to the rules of insurance.

But since a believing Muslim wants to practise his religion and, for example, conceal his wife (although the Koran does not prescribe headscarves or hijab), he would not feel at all comfortable in such an environment. It is also impossible for him to then demand the so-called jizya, a kind of punitive tax, from unbelievers. Today the state's transfers serve as jizya, so that for many Muslims it is quite natural that unbelievers work hard for them. That is why some of them are so impudent to the government agencies that even they doubt whether this culture is compatible with Western culture.

Even a bleeding-heart refugee worker told the "Welt" newspaper on 17 January 2016 that many asylum seekers were "extremely demanding, unreliable and obtrusive". This is not limited to Muslims, but most illegal immigrants come from Muslim countries. African immigrants are probably persuaded by left-wing organisations that they have a right to free all-round care because of colonisation. Those are recommended to compare the conditions during colonial times with those of today.

Islam would either completely reform itself or disappear from areas with a private legal system. There is even a certain chance of rapprochement because Sharia law in principle represents a private legal order in which respected judges — imams — speak the law. However, the law is hopelessly out of date. But the more radical currents of Islam insist that these old rules be implemented in a literal way. This is particularly successful in states, as can now be seen from 57 examples. For once they have climbed to the top of the state there, these radical groups rule. In Western countries, on the other hand, left-wing radical groups have meanwhile conquered the leadership and are not taking action against the spread of Islam, but are even promoting it, although there is no equality for women, anti-Semitism and open hatred of gays there.

It is not unlikely that a moderate version of Islam would prevail even in Islamic regions without a state, because then the same economic laws that I am describing here would apply. But in any case, in areas that are not yet predominantly Muslim, a respective process of civilization would immediately begin. However, Western countries are currently working flat out to create an irreversible situation.

Back to the no-go area: Suppose an insured person was willing to pay her premium and is raped by a member of a gang. As a rule, gang members proceed carelessly because they were used to getting away with it. So in our example you would know exactly who it was, and you would also know that he is a member of a gang and probably a serial criminal.

The insurance could price in that the victim of the crime now gets a lifelong pension, which allows her to move out of the No-Go-Area. This doesn't create a big moral hazard problem, such as that many victims would now fake rapes, because after all the potential perpetrator will try to defend himself in court. The contract could also include severe penalties for false accusations.

The insurance company would now commission a special squad to get the insured out and arrest the perpetrator. The special squad would ensure that collateral damage is kept to a minimum. The professionals do not want to harm other insured persons or potential customers. The gang members are all not insured anyway, the procedure might be rougher there.

As soon as the gang member is in the power of the special squad, they retreat. He is brought before an anonymous judge in an entirely different place. Today gang members learn the name of the judge, he usually lives nearby and unprotected. Don't forget: The gang member has no insurance, he has to accept the conditions of the court company. In contrast to previously innocent citizens, it would leave such a person with few options. The perpetrator would be locked away for a long time, but in an unknown place.

Today, he would join his buddies in the slammer, which is usually also already controlled by the local gangs. Just think of the "scandal" within the Berlin police. Not only is it obviously infiltrated by gang members. Even previously convicted got their way before a state court when they filed a lawsuit against exclusion from the police service! Completely unthinkable in a PLS.

How could the gangs react now, who would surely be terribly angry? They would neither know the members of the special squad nor which company they belonged to. They would only know — if at all — where the victim was insured.

What are they going to do? Storm a huge billion-dollar corporation based on the other side of the world? Good luck with that! Complain to the press that one of their brutal gang members was kidnapped? Again: Good luck with that!

If you are still afraid at this point that private security companies would deal with innocent citizens in the same way, that is not the case. They would be insured by another large company and there would certainly be an outcry in the press with the danger of losing all customers. But no ordinary citizen would be at all bothered if there was one less felon on the streets.

And there wouldn't be any motive to treat an uninsured average citizen like that. Of course, you can again construct some lifeboat scenarios that somehow an innocent person would be caught up in. But that's the normal case today! Just think of the many thousands of crime victims today. There is no absolute security for everything and everyone. The only thing that can always be done is to reduce risks as much as possible.

Why would a corporation even care about a no-go area like this? Here we are again on the subject of specialization. Cleaning up such areas is a huge business. Those who are successful can win a lion's share of the honest citizens there as customers. Some insurance companies or some security companies will concentrate on this, perhaps because the owner himself comes from such a region and has a special motive for helping other victims. That's how the market works.

Initially, the companies would certainly concentrate on the easy areas, similar to today's private cities or gated communities that are built more for the well-off. But at some point, however, a company will concentrate on this market, especially when the easy areas are already largely developed. This can be observed everywhere, even in urban planning. Once some companies have decided to invest in a certain area, others follow suit and the better buildings spread.

The way to get really rich is through the mass of customers, therefore the Aldi (supermarket) brothers belong to the richest Germans. So even if the richer customers are targeted first, it can't be long before the benefits of PLS reach the masses.

I suppose it would look like this: Once a company has cleaned up a no-go area, it becomes much easier to do so in the other no-go areas. The company could go and say to the gangs of the other areas, "Look, we cleaned up area XY. You have 24 hours to leave the area or become honest and insure yourself." This insurance would be expensive, of course. But it is in the nature of gangs that many of them take part for self-protection but would prefer to be honest. They could be given a second chance, as explained above, but with appropriate security measures. If someone proves himself, the premiums decrease, similarly as with beginner drivers in the course of time.

Even if you think the above scenario is unrealistic: You have to again see the difference with regard to the state. The police are pulling out of the no-go areas because there's nothing to gain. If they withdraw, the crimes committed there do not appear in any statistics. Therefore the state denies almost everywhere that such areas exist at all. But all you have to do is read about it in the mainstream press under the keyword "No-Go-Areas". They're spreading extremely fast. That is a fact that can no longer be denied. If the police dare to go into such an area, the policemen very quickly end up before a state court, which, for ideological reasons or because it is afraid of the gangs, gives the police a harder time than the criminals.

In a PLS it would be exactly the opposite for economic reasons: it would be the "Go-Areas", i.e. the civilized areas, that spread. Again, I can only recommend that you ask a police officer. He'll confirm what I've said.

The end of the Mafia

One of the biggest problems in any state is of course the mafia. For many reasons, it would simply disappear. What are the Mafia's main areas of business? Prostitution, gambling, drugs, money laundering and extortion. The first four transactions would be legal in a PLS, so all that would remain is the extortion of protection money. This would make the Mafia a normal competitor of the other security companies, but with significant disadvantages.

First of all, it must be understood that the mafia cannot exist without the state. If the state did not prohibit certain transactions, they would be normal business activities. But it goes much deeper than that. Unlike thieves and murderers, the mafia needs customers for their core businesses. But this also means that it is very easy to bust the deal.

Just as during the prohibition everyone knew in which bars alcohol was served, today everyone can go to any club in any country at any time, ask for drugs and get them. A policeman just has to do the same, follow the dealer to his middleman and finally to the boss. A ten-year-old could do that.

It follows logically that the mafia must have the judiciary in its hands, and since it is a monopoly, it must ultimately buy only one institution. The historical facts prove it. Before the "Cosa Nostra"'s cover was blown in America, FBI chief Hoover had categorically denied that there was a mafia. Hoover was a Mason, by the way. In the chapter on the power of lodges, you will see that this is not surprising. Chance would have it that a foot patrol officer became aware of a meeting of the fine society. After the local police raided the nest, it turned out that the Mafia had bribed politicians, judges and police. Because that's exactly what their business model has to be.

Everyone knew, for example, that Al Capone was a mafia boss, and this became a growing problem for politicians. That he was finally caught for tax evasion is probably due to the fact that this way he could be taken out of circulation without all his collaborators in police and the judiciary being exposed. The strict drug laws essentially serve to keep private competition out of the market.

The state itself, in the USA especially the secret service CIA, is the biggest drug smuggler. Even the New York Times wrote on 3 December 1993 that the CIA had been involved in drug trafficking since its inception. Pulitzer Prize winner Gary Webb wrote about it in books and articles. He is said to have killed himself in 2004, with two shots in the head! It is obvious that he was killed, and the monopolist on the use of force naturally covers this murder because he is the criminal, that is to say, he himself is involved in the conflict.

In a PLS, the Mafia would have to have all insurance and court companies in its hands. I have already described how such corruption — which is practically impossible anyway — can be prevented in individual cases. All that would remain for the Mafia to do would be extortion of protection money anyway. But here, too, the problem for the Mafia is that this is a crime that is particularly easy to prosecute. The Mafioso has to collect the protection money and at that moment a special squad would be waiting for him, which would be sent by the voluntarily summoned protection organization.

I would like to take this opportunity to remind you of the economic interrelationships that apply similarly to the no-go areas. Suppose the Mafia controlled an area the size of Schwabing with his 100.000 citizens. A security company begins to take an interest in the area and prepares a market analysis. For example, it concludes that, as in the example above, it would cost about ten euros per month per citizen to keep order once the area has been cleared of the Mafia, gangs and habitual criminals.

The company evaluates what value the residents would place on getting rid of the Mafia. I suppose you will agree with me that EUR 100 per month per citizen would not be too high a price to pay. Of course, the company must also anticipate the market share. We simply assume that an average of EUR 100 per citizen could be achieved. Let us also assume that the company predicts that it would be possible to establish five-year contracts. What would the calculation look like then?

100 euros per month per citizen would be 120 million euros a year in an area like Schwabing with 100,000 inhabitants, minus the ten euros of long-term costs, i.e. a possible yield of 108 million euros. Of course, in the long run, the revenues would level off towards ten euros plus the profit margin, because the area would become safer and competitors would enter. But for five years, about 540 million euros could be earned.

The company could come to the conclusion that it would be worthwhile investing ten million euros in the fight against the mafia. That would only need to go well in one out of ten cases and it would be profitable after the first year. How could the ten million be used? They could pay informants, offer a new life to accomplice witnesses, or even make an offer to the mafia boss to quit. The latter would seriously disturb our sense of justice and perhaps it would be cheaper to eliminate him, but I just want to show you the options here. Clearing up by force involves risks, so this option will certainly be taken into consideration.

No matter how it is done: In the end, citizens will be safer. They may not know anything about a possible deal with the Mafia boss. But wouldn't the security company be the new mob? No, because it would be insured by a large company, which would of course observe all its actions. If it allowed the emergence of a new mafia, it would lose all its customers worldwide to the competition, which is limited to protecting its customers.

Again, you must see the difference with regard to the state: It wouldn't have such options, even if it wanted to. But as we have seen, as a monopolist it has no interest in them anyway. On the contrary, the representatives of the state are involved in organised crime and can also enforce better surveillance measures, which in reality serve to monitor the tax slave.

Another good example is the Mafia's latest business sector: the overpriced rental of real estate to "refugees". Without the state, this business model wouldn't exist. And since the Mafia has the politicians on their pay roll anyway, they can get their bribe recipients to approve the real estate and to give them the orders. That is why this is a classic field of employment for the mafia, of course in other European countries as well. The stupid tax slave pays.

Don't cling to the specific figures, these are just examples to illustrate the economic effects. You should see that it is definitely a lucrative business to sort out the Mafia or No-Go-Areas. In reality, therefore, the harassed citizens will be swamped with offers from security companies, which of course drives down prices to such an extent that it would be lucrative enough to take the risk. This is how every market works in every industry.

Nor should you forget that the top of the mafia is made up of professionals who know markets, risks, the production of security and legal systems like hardly any other organization. The mafia also has its own jurisdiction. This is one of the most important functions of the "godfather". Since the Mafia operates outside of state laws, it naturally needs very special regulations that legal companies do not need. Treason, for example, is punishable by death.

The mafia is also constantly confronted with territorial disputes. If, for example, a member of another Mafia crosses the virtual borders, this must be punished. As a rule, you then sit down with the competing Mafia boss. If both belong to the same organization, the boss above them decides.

Sometimes somebody has to be punished, nevertheless. The Mexican and presumably other Mafias have ensured that the sanction will also be enforced if the border transgressor goes to prison. They have their people in all prisons, but if there is no killer of their own on the spot, another organization is commissioned to do it. This is the bounty payment system described.

Even pirates had their own legal system. In order to protect themselves from despotic captains, sailors of a pirate ship could later bring them to court (cf. Peter Leeson: "Pirates, Prisoners, and Preliterates: Anarchic Context and the Private Enforcement of Law"). So you can see quite clearly here: even for people who obviously do not believe in property rights because they are thieves, rights arise simply because they themselves are interested in them.

Since the Mafia understands this system very well, they also know that they have no chance against a private security organization. In the state it can bribe the monopolist. This is not possible in a PLS, as I have explained several times. It has all ordinary citizens, all security companies and billion-dollar insurance companies against it, instead of a few corrupt and weak politicians.

Since the Mafia is always laundering money anyway, i.e. transferring it to legal companies, it would simply withdraw to the legal business. It is possible that part of the organisation may actually remain as a security service provider. A certain amount of expertise is available. By the way, the Sicilian mafia demanded about five percent of the turnover for its protection services. This is considerably cheaper than the state, because the mafia cannot become too expensive for reasons of competition. If this business becomes legal, the prices will just go down even further. The Mafia will be a normal competitor.

There are already indications that the Mafia is taking over state functions where the state is so totally failing that the Mafia is losing its "customers" because they are all moving away or because they fear competition. In Naples, the Camorra is said to have shot 120 Africans in the head. This figure can only be found in alternative media, but the Daily Mail also reported on 23 April 2016 about a bloody war of the Cosa Nostra against the "refugees". The shooting of an African by a Mafia member is even documented with pictures.

In a private law system, however, a non-criminal company would win in the end. The Mafia dissolves or becomes a normal security company. Employees of the former criminal mafia who do not adapt to the market, i.e. work honestly, would probably be sorted out by the godfather himself. Such purging processes of people who are too aggressive already exist today. This process would, of course, accelerate rapidly if the Mafia were faced with an invincible opponent. Therefore, the transition would probably be quite bloodless. This also applies to the following groups, which are ultimately just a mafia as well.

The end of the deep state

With the state, of course, the deep state too ceases to exist. How is the deep state defined even according to mainstream representation, i.e. Wikipedia?

The term deep state (Turkish: derin devlet) is used in Turkey in the meaning of a state within the state. It points to a conspiratorial integration of the military, secret services, politicians, the judiciary, administration, right-wing extremism and organized crime (especially killer squads) that has grown over several decades.

In the left-wing Wikipedia, of course, the emphasis is on right-wing extremism, but that's nonsense, of course. What is meant is any kind of terrorism, most of which, in almost every state, comes from the left or Islam at the moment. But you must realize that no such entanglement can exist without a state, because the conflict decision-maker is not a party to the conflict. The crimes of the deep state are always covered by the monopolist on the use of force. At this point you should already be concerned with "false flag"-operations, but this is not the subject of this book. Nevertheless, I would like to show you what would happen in a PLS by means of an officially busted secret lodge.

The power of the lodges would be broken

With regard to this, here a short excerpt from my book „Die Vereinigten Staaten von Europa" about the P2-Lodge (You can find the original sources there, but you can also research it yourself):

The boss of this lodge (master of the chair), Licio Gelli, is where all the threads come together. He was a member of the Order of Malta, the Order of Knights of the Holy Sepulchre in Jerusalem, a Freemason, and worked with the Nazi organization Odessa. But that's not all. Regine Igel writes in her book „Terrorjahre" (Terror Years):

It was Ted Shackly, director of all CIA covert operations in Italy in the 1970s, who introduced the head of the P2 Masonic Lodge, Alexander Haig (Maltese Knight). In autumn 1969, Haig and Kissinger gave Gelli the authority to recruit 400 high Italian and NATO officers to his lodge.

A report by the Observer of 18 November 1990 confirms this. CIA agent Richard Brennecke explained in an interview with Italian RAI journalist Ennio Remondino that the P2 lodge had been financed by the CIA. Another member of the P2 Lodge and the Order of Malta was Roberto Calvi, who became known as the "God's Banker", did business with the Vatican Bank and was found hanged on 18 June 1982 in London under the Blackfriars Bridge and, according to a trial that took place in 2005 (!), murdered.

In his book „La Repubblica delle stragi impunite" (2012), the former anti-mafia judge Ferdinando Imposimato describes the alliance between the Mafia, Freemasonry, Gladio and secret services and accuses the Bilderbergers of being directly involved in the terrorist acts of Gladio. There can't be a more credible witness. Imposimato risked his life to fight the Mafia.

P2-member Silvio Berlusconi became prime minister several times after the ban of the lodge. What's more, in 2003 Licio Gelli boasted in the daily La Repubblica that Berlusconi was gradually putting all his plans into practice. Henry Kissinger and the CIA were never prosecuted.

So we see that the mafia, the deep state, certain lodges, these are ultimately only different names for malicious organizations that exert influence on the state. Whatever you believe about who influences the state, be it secret lodges, lobbyists, corporations, banks, malicious super villains or the devil himself, in a PRG there is no violent monopolist who could be influenced in this way. Let's make it concrete:

So we have a malicious organization, let's call it the Illuminati for fun, but you can also call it Mafia or Cosa Nostra (which actually means "our thing" and was never the Mafia's proper name). What evil can the Illuminati do in a PLS? Let's take terrorist attacks: The aim of the terrorist attacks, and this has even been officially admitted in the case of Gladio, is to increase people's sense of insecurity so that they accept a surveillance state and a weapons bans. Congratulations, great plan!

In a PLS, insurance companies would even offer discounts to customers who arm themselves. So the demand for weapons would increase and not the call for bans, because there would be no state that could ban anything. There would only be insurance companies with an interest in armed and well-trained customers because they would have to pay less for damages.

Surveillance: As shown, there would also be some degree of monitoring in a PLS, but only where it makes sense. The best way to illustrate this is to look at the difference between controls at airports and shopping malls. At the airport, some pervert will reach between your legs or send you through a radioactive body scanner. I would have loved to have polished the face of one or the other sex offender at the airport, but of course I hold back, because in a state there is no other way to fly.

In most developing countries, there are checks at the entrances of shopping centres, and in Germany this will probably soon be the case. But since the shopping centre has an interest in customers, its security guards are exceptionally friendly and will give you directions if necessary. You will hardly ever be frisked, and certainly never between your legs. Only if you come up with the clever idea of taking a backpack with you does the security guard want to take a look inside. In gated communities even this is usually omitted, because checks took place at the entrance and one knows the people.

But couldn't that be exactly the aim of attacks? To sell more guns or build a state? In order to do this, one has to understand that the military-industrial complex forms a unity with the state. In a PLS, the arms manufacturer has several opponents: security companies would ensure that the arms manufacturer does not build weapons of mass destruction. Insurers would never allow their customers to buy from uninsured manufacturers. These would have to undergo controls and would be monitored in turn. So if a weapons manufacturer or whoever were really to carry out an attack he would be more efficiently pursued. And, of course, the insurance company would make sure that the neutral judge was not paid by the offender.

Apart from that, the arms manufacturer would not even know that precisely his weapons would be bought in response to an attack. If the deep state carries out an attack, it is clear from the outset who will then receive the orders to arm the security apparatus, because the perpetrator is identical with the client and the latter with the contractor.

But what if in a PLS the malicious organization secretly bribes all neutral judges? First of all, it's virtually impossible. Secondly, as I have already described, there are sufficient countermeasures. But let's assume the judge is in some nasty, super-secret organization. When the first wrong judgement is made, he is busted, as is the secret organization as well. You can imagine the punishments. In a state these organizations' cover is hardly ever blown, because the organization only has to take control of the monopolist.

And there's an example from England. The Mirror wrote on 23 November 2015 under the headline "How secret group of Freemasons has kept grip on Britain for 200 years":

The huge influence Freemasons had in ruling British society for almost 200 years has finally been revealed. The names of royalty, statesmen, judges, military top brass, bishops and police have been found in a secret archive which lists two million Freemasons.

The Mirror correctly writes that the history books must be rewritten. The archive ends in 1923, but the author does not claim that the influence of the Freemasons also ended there. The public only doesn't know today's members. The history books also don't say whether this group was smashed at some point. The Mirror even reported that the Masons sabotaged the Titanic and Jack the Ripper investigations.

How great the influence still is today can easily be proven. The <u>Daily Mail</u> wrote on 8 March 2008 that the Duke of Kent *is head of the secret organisation — he is Grand Master of the United Grand Lodge of England.*

On 22 March 2015, the <u>Daily Mail</u> also reported that in the 1980s Scotland Yard had suspended and concealed investigations into a gigantic paedophile ring involving celebrities from the judiciary, politics and the media for "national security reasons". Among the suspects was a *mysterious member of the royal family.*

Officially, Buckingham Palace can't stop an investigation, so it's quite clear that the influence was exerted through the very Masonic lodges that the Duke of Kent is in charge of and whose ranks are obviously made up of pedophiles who have been protected here.

At this point you should ask yourself why the governments of other countries do not address and denounce this influence of Freemasons on UK politics. The answer is obvious: because exactly the same networks exist there. For Germany, this influence is clearly demonstrable. I already show this in my English book "New World Order exposed" and soon also in a German book. Here are just a few brief hints.

Angela Merkel accepted the <u>Coudenhove-Kalergi Prize in</u> 2011. The Freemason wrote in 1925 in his book Practical Idealism:

The man of the distant future will be a hybrid. Today's races and castes will fall victim to the increasing overcoming of space, time and prejudice. The Eurasian-Negroid future race, externally similar to the ancient Egyptian one, will replace the diversity of peoples with a diversity of personalities.

Coudenhove-Kalergi also added:

The influence of the blood aristocracy decreases, the influence of the spirit aristocracy grows. This development, and with it the chaos of modern politics, will only then come to an end until a spiritual aristocracy seizes the means of power of society: powder, gold and printing ink and uses them for the blessing of the general public.

You can, in the end, also read about these principles of the exercise of power in Machiavelli. Coudenhove-Kalergi has only very succinctly summarised how Freemasons or other interest groups exert this influence: Through the monopoly of power (powder), the control of the monetary system (gold) and the press (printing ink). This, too, is surprisingly easy to prove:

The founder of the second largest publishing house in Germany, Axel Springer, was a member of the Masonic Lodge "Die Brückenbauer". Thomas Dehler, a former Minister of Justice (!) according to Freimaurer-Wiki (not a "conspiracy page", but operated by Freemasons) is quoted in a commemorative publication of the Brückenbauer in conversation with Theodor Vogel, the initiator of the first umbrella organization of the German grand lodges:

We must contribute Masonic ideas to the construction of the Federal Republic of Germany. The best thing would be for us to unite those responsible in a lodge.

Liz Mohn, the head of Germany's largest media group, was the first female member of Rockefeller's Club of Rome. The Rockefellers in turn officially allied themselves with the Rothschilds in 2012. About this family writes the Israeli mainstream newspaper "Israel National News":

The Supreme Court building in Jerusalem, notes Chomsky, was built in 1992, with funding that had been offered by the Yad Hanadiv foundation. Many members of the Rothschild family, which owns Yad Hanadiv, were proud members of the Freemasons, she says.

Chomsky refers to the mainstream journalist Gilit Chomsky.

Jacob Rothschild in turn is a member of the Royal Order of Merit and knight of the Knight Grand Cross of the Order of the British Empire. Do you see any connections here?

It should be clear to you by now at the latest that these influential groups are merging with the state to form a unity, the deep state. No matter how big you consider this influence to be, this is not possible in a PLS because the judge must not be a party to the conflict. It would, of course, still be possible to infiltrate individual court companies, but as soon as obviously incorrect judgments are made, customers would switch. I have already explained this in several places, but here is another case that even made it into the mainstream press. The Süddeutsche Zeitung wrote on 4 June 2013 about the Gustl Mollath case:

In the committee of inquiry on Gustl Mollath, one learns strange things about the habits of the Nuremberg Rotary Club. Klaus Hubmann, 67, is summoned as a witness, before his retirement he was Attorney General in Nuremberg, the highest representative of the prosecuting authority. However, the committee now asks him about his Rotary club membership. And Hubmann confirms, yes, when the public prosecutor's office received the first reports about ten years ago, he had the honor of being president of the Rotarians. And yes, the local Rotary clubs were administered from a room in the branch building of the Hypo-Vereinsbank (HVB).

Let's just repeat that again: The highest representative of the prosecution in the case of Mollath, a man who was committed to psychiatry because he uncovered a very real conspiracy of the Hypovereinsbank, was president of the association that had an office in a branch of that bank! And even though this is in the press and came to light at a parliamentary committee of inquiry, neither the prosecutor, nor the judge, nor the consultant are behind bars!

On May 23, 1983, Der Spiegel wrote that Rotarians and Lions (Lions Club) *made up a solid third of the CDU, CSU, and FDP boards.* Mollath was convicted in 2006. The Bavarian Minister of the Interior at the time was Rotarian Günther Beckstein, who was also prime minister from 2007 to 2008. We remember that the public prosecutor's office in Germany is completely officially instruction-bound to the government. Afterwards Horst Seehofer followed, who is even author for the Rotary magazine. Minister of Justice Beate Merk served under both. She is a member of the Rotary Club Ulm/Neu-Ulm. Even the Süddeutsche Zeitung considered it to be cynical that Merk commended herself for the release of Mollath, although she did everything she could to prevent it. She said these sentences before about Mollath:

"I have to assume that he's rightly in a psychiatric ward."

"Mr. Mollath is dangerous. One of the reasons for this was that he committed serious bodily injuries to his wife. The court has established it on the basis of expert opinions."

"He's in psychiatric treatment because he's dangerous."

It didn't hurt her career. She became Minister of European Affairs. But already in 2014 she had the next scandal attached to her. She was accused in the "Handelsblatt" of 21.11.2014, among others, of having failed to prosecute at least ten thousand doctors for fraudulent settlements during her time as Minister of Justice. Doctors are particularly welcome members of Rotarians because they do so much good. In April 2014, Rotarians proudly reported that one of their members, doctor Melanie Huml, was the youngest state minister in Seehofer's cabinet. There she is responsible for the medical profession as "Minister for Health and Nursing Care".

That's provincial politics, of course. Freemason lodges are obviously responsible for big politics, as the example of England shows.

In a PLS, Mollath – within the framework of the procedure described by me — could not only have chosen the court company, he could now also retrospectively take legal action against the perpetrators, who had robbed him of his freedom, at any court. The first court company would lose all its customers and the perpetrators would be liable for damages. Of course, it is precisely for this reason that a court company would ensure that such conflicts of interest do not arise in the first place. Today, Mollath can only complain to the same institution that kidnapped him and robbed him of his freedom.

The instrument with which Mollath was to be neutralized also deserves a closer look. He was imprisoned by the expert consultant and the judge because he allegedly suffered from a "paranoid personality disorder". According to the guideline ICD10 issued by the World Health Organization (WHO), one characteristic is the

frequent preoccupation with unfounded thoughts of conspiracies as explanations for events in the immediate or wider environment.

Thus the state can lock away every "conspiracy theorist" forever. Because who should decide whether these thoughts are "unfounded"? The state also claims that critics of the ridiculous official theory of September 11 (cf. my other books and my "Focus Money" articles on it) are putting out unfounded "conspiracy theories".

Mollath, for example, had uncovered a very real conspiracy. Of course, in a PLS nobody can be locked away because of his thoughts, but only if a plaintiff can prove that he has suffered specific damages. But states can and do imprison any unpopular person in this way. Just find out how many people are being sent into psychiatric care because of this "disease", even though they haven't done any harm to anyone.

The European Court of Human Rights provided a prime example of what we are in for with increasing centralization. In the nineties, the British press increasingly reported on the dangerous activities of questionable Masonic lodges. The British press is much freer than the German press, as you can see from the fact that these scandals were not reported in the German press at all or only very sparsely. The state broadcaster BBC reported on March 9, 2012 that in 1999 things had gone too far even for the British state and it demanded that judges disclose whether they belonged to a Masonic lodge. That is only right and proper, because judges hold a public office, not a secret one. In 2009, the European Court of Human Rights overturned this rule and ruled that judges could do so voluntarily and only to their superiors.

Three guesses as to who is controlling this Court and who would control a World Court. Here, too, we can see why we are moving toward increasing centralization: Because then only one central institution has to be controlled. In a PLS, there would be thousands of independent court companies voluntarily elected. Of course, customers could turn to court companies that also require disclosure of lodge memberships and impose severe penalties should membership be concealed.

In a PLS there is always a powerful opponent who represents the mass of customers. This becomes particularly clear with an issue that has so far been completely beyond any control:

The end of geoengineering and mind control

Mainstream media such as Der Spiegel on 9 October 2017 now report quite openly on a topic that was long regarded as a "conspiracy theory": geoengineering, i.e. technologies to influence the weather. As early as 13 July 1995, a European Parliament session called for a ban on weather weapons and other technologies to influence the weather and people. It literally says, among other things, that the Committee

calls, in particular, for an international agreement banning research and development projects, whether military or civil, which involve the use of knowledge in the field of chemical and electrical processes or of sound waves or other functions of the human brain to develop weapons which could open the door to any form of human manipulation, to be universally banned; this agreement should also include a ban on all known and conceivable uses of such systems (...).

So although even state bodies have dealt with the issue, it has not been reported, nor has any ban been imposed.

How would that be dealt with in a PLS? The obvious opponents of such organizations are, of course, the insurance companies, the very large ones, because they are liable with huge sums for the damage caused by storms or even for influencing the human brain (mind control).

We're talking about billions here. What percentage of these billions do you think insurance companies would use to eliminate this danger? It is possible that a public deterrent judicial procedure would be put in place for the operators of such installations. But maybe they would just let these mass murderers disappear.

But why don't insurers fight back today? If today an insurer were to denounce these events or even prosecute the operators, the state would withdraw its licence, the disseminators of the information would be killed and state judges would cover these crimes.

It's the other way around: the fact that insurers do nothing is proof that they themselves are part of the system. You want more proof? The largest reinsurance company in the world, Munich Re, i.e. the one that suffers the greatest losses when geoengineering is used, cooperates with the Club of Rome. So this is exactly the Rockefeller association that is trying to convince us that the common people influence the climate through the production of CO_2 and not (in this case even directly by state operated) plants like HAARP, which are explicitly mentioned in the EU report:

27. considers HAARP (High Frequency Active Auroral Research Project) to be a global issue because of its far-reaching environmental impact and calls for the legal, environmental and ethical implications to be investigated by an independent international body before further research and experimentation takes place; regrets the repeated refusal of the US Government to send a representative to the public hearing or subsequent meetings of its competent committee on the effects of the High Frequency Active Auroral Research Project (HAARP) currently being conducted in Alaska;

28. calls on the STOA (Scientific and Technological Options Assessment) steering group to agree that the scientific and technical evidence available in all available research on HAARP should be examined to determine the precise nature and hazard potential of HAARP for both the local and global environment and for human health in general;

29. calls on the Commission, in cooperation with the governments of Sweden, Finland, Norway and the Russian Federation, to study the impact of the HAARP programme on the Arctic regions of Europe from the point of view of the environment and public health and to report to Parliament on the results (...).

I have already reported in many places about the alleged man-made climate change, therefore here only briefly the facts with reference to my other books:

There is no correlation between CO_2 and temperature and no experiment, so there is no connection. Even if there were one, the human contribution to annual CO_2 emissions is low at 1.2 percent and the contribution of CO_2 to the atmosphere is tiny at 0.04 percent.

Obviously, however, there are technologies to influence the weather and it is precisely these that are not outlawed. At the same time, politicians and the media are blaming the average citizen for climate change in order to be able to control his whole lifestyle, since CO_2 is produced in practically every production process and during exhalation. As seen above, the real environmental problems would be regulated by insurance. If someone pollutes a river, for example, this affects all residents and groundwater users. Those who are affected could sue, with billion-dollar insurances behind them.

A recent example of how insurance companies act, if they are allowed to, is 5G. Lloyds of London, one of the world's premier insurance groups, is refusing to insure health claims made against 5G wireless ("wi-fi") technologies. Whereas governments assume these risks with taxpayers' money.

The end of all wars

From everything you have read so far, you can con-clude that there can be no more wars in a worldwide PLS. Only states wage wars with forcibly collected taxes. In a PLS, there would be no territory to conquer. Wars in a PLS are expensive and pointless. As already explained, it would be idiotic to occupy the head office of an insurance company, for example, because cus-tomers would then no longer pay.

At best there would still be regional conflicts if local gangs in no-go areas behaved unreasonably and did not give up immediately. This is, of course, nothing compared to the more than one hundred million dead, including many civilians, that state wars have cost so far.

Interestingly, even those who openly strive for world government justify their goal by ending all wars. But it should be clear that a world government means a per-manent war against the population. Imagine a single central institution able to decide about your fate. You can't even flee to another country from excessively high taxes or other harassment. Absolute power cor-rupts absolutely. It would indeed be as George Orwell once put it in "1984":

If you want a picture of the future, imagine a boot stamping on a human face — forever.

New technologies

Technologies can always be used for good or for bad. There are numerous indications that technologies have existed for a long time that would further mankind a great deal. But the (deep) state prevents this in two ways. First, by granting patents that would not exist in a PLS. This way, that knowledge is obtained by the state. The state can prohibit the use of technology for "reasons of national security". The American government, for example, keeps over 5,000 patents secret. This means that neither the inventor nor anyone else can officially use these patents. But of course the clandestine groups within the deep state can access them.

Secondly, should an inventor dare to not apply for a patent at all or simply publish his results, he will be sent to prison or killed. The state covers up these crimes. There are countless examples of this. I just want to pick a very prominent one here, because there is even a German film worth seeing about it: Wilhelm Reich. This inventor was not only temporarily imprisoned, but, according to the film, even forced by apparently sadistically inclined FBI officials to destroy his inventions himself.

I have no idea if his equipment really works, but in a PLS such a thing would not only be unthinkable, inventors would be much better protected. In a PLS, an inventor would only be punished if he contractually assures a characteristic of his invention which it subsequently does not have. Nobody will do this with medical devices, because a healing success is always uncertain. But independent agencies could run tests and publish them. These could in turn be sued if it can be shown that the tests were performed fraudulently.

In the case of energy production equipment, on the other hand, the production of a certain amount of energy could easily be assured. This could easily be reviewed by a court of law. The case of the German physicist Prof. Claus Turtur shows that the state deliberately blocks such inventions. He claims in his book „Freie Energie für alle Menschen: Raumenergiemotor: Nachweis und Bauanleitung" (Free energy for all: Spatial energy motor: Proof and construction manual) and elsewhere that he had proved experimentally that such a form of energy (also called zero point energy or vacuum energy) actually exists. He wrote to federal chancellor Angela Merkel that he only needed two or three million euros to publicly repeat the experiment in a laboratory with expensive equipment (and not as in his "homemade" experiment) and build a prototype. His request was denied. Why spend tens of billions of euros on ancient technologies such as windmills when only a few million would be enough for a much better technology?

Now one could object that Turtur may have falsified his own test results. But that wasn't proven at all. His request was simply denied. In his book Turtur also describes the case of the inventor Prof. Stefan Marinow, who is said to have jumped off the roof of the University of Graz shortly after the successful presentation of a spatial energy converter. The official cause of death found on Wikipedia is actually "suicide in Graz".

Of course, it is ridiculous to assume that someone will jump off the roof after a successful presentation. But even if you argue that this successful presentation may not have existed at all, it seems very unlikely that such a researcher would simply kill himself, even if he has not yet made the breakthrough. Here, too, we can see quite clearly that it is the state that at least blocks a clarification of the case, but most probably deliberately conceals a crime. At the very least, one should expect that any research results would be made public: Nothing.

How would that be in a PLS? Well, an inventor could just insure himself for a large sum. As we have seen, insurance to solve murder cases costs only about ten cents for ten million euros. Even if this figure were too low, he could simply insure himself for 100 million or a billion. Of course, in this case the insurance company would check exactly who that is, so it might be smarter to take a normal sum. If it were determined that the inventor was at risk, the premium would probably be raised. However, it would in no case be significant compared to the investment costs of a venture capitalist. There would also certainly be insurance and security companies specialising in inventors.

Turtur wonders in his book why he can't find venture capitalists. The reason should now be clear: A little research would show that all those who claimed to have invented such a machine have died prematurely. A professional would of course know immediately that they were killed and that the state protects the perpetrators. The risk is far too high. I cannot deal with the subject exhaustively here, but since I have been researching it for a very long time, let me say this much: if this technology exists, the big companies have already had it for a long time, so it makes no sense for a small supplier to go on the market at all. As soon as the technology was officially recognised, they would immediately launch the products on the market. Today they are not doing so because the conventional energy companies have the state in their pockets. You can even read critical articles in the mainstream press about the influence of the oil industry on political decisions. A venture capitalist therefore has little prospect of return, but the maximum risk of being murdered.

The same applies of course to the discoverers of alternative and natural remedies. Doctors who use them often lose their licence to practise medicine, end up in prison or die prematurely. This is of course due to the influence of the pharmaceutical industry, which cannot patent natural remedies. Here too, in a PLS, the insurers would be the opponents who would be nationalized today if, for example, they were to do without state-approved drugs.

And for the clever-clogs who always appear when the subject is energy, even though they have not researched it like I have for more than ten years, I have another remark: This technology does not violate the law of conservation of energy. Where the energy comes from, however, you will have to research yourself. This is possible on the basis of publicly available information. However, I can assure you and the psychopaths of the deep state that I do not conduct research on such devices and if you request I will not establish contacts or provide further information. We can talk about that when the state is abolished. I'm not suicidal.

The mere fact that inventors would obviously be better protected in a PLS would probably catapult mankind a hundred years forward technologically, if the state were abolished. Just think of the work of Nikola Tesla. This much I can tell you: Tesla wasn't a crank, he was a genius. He was sabotaged by the perfect example of a corporatist and robber baron: J.P. Morgan, who was also jointly responsible for the establishment of the Federal Reserve. You will learn little about this in the mass stupefaction media, whose harmful influence would practically disappear in a PLS:

The end of the lying press

Under the pretext of fighting "hate speech", the state is trying to make it as difficult as possible for alternative media. Especially in Germany, state broadcasters are courting the "quality media" with forcibly collected TV-license billions and denigrating alternative competitors as "fake news". That the secret services infiltrate the media is also a proven fact. Alternative media would therefore have an easier life without the state. Nor would there be a fiat money system that would allow large banks to buy themselves into the media. But even if all the groups that control the media today did the same in a PLS, the impact would be small.

For example, the big media could continue to spread climate propaganda all the time, but no one could force you to buy expensive electricity from windmills. Since there is no politics, the big media would have no choice but to report on consumer protection, i.e. the quality of companies. When something's being sugar-coated, it's quickly noticed. As is already the case today, there would be innumerable competitors and independent test companies, which would test the quality of most products; except that without the state there would naturally be much more demand for such test companies. This also increases the competitive pressure and quality for them compared to today.

Just think about what the media will want to tell you in the future that would specifically influence your life? Today, the media try to influence you to vote for a particular party (from the party cartel) or rather not to vote for it (if it is not part of the cartel). Whoever wins in the end rules all. But that is not the question in a PLS.

Everyone can choose for himself who represents his interests, and if the supplier does not do it well, the customer just switches suppliers. The interests of the readers are always represented by a freely chosen company, which at the same time represents the interests of millions of others.

The media could also try to persuade you day and night that there is no difference between the sexes, or that some marginalised groups are terribly discriminated against. It would have no effect, because you yourself decide with whom you maintain contact or whether you, as a publican, install a toilet for the 0.01 percent of the population who do not know whether they are male or female. A PLS also means the end of all ideologies. In any case, they would not be subsidized by the state because there would be no state-funded universities. But if crazy billionaires still wanted to spread such fairy tales, this would remain a harmless hobby that would have no effect on your life.

The minarchist, the strangest species on the planet

The strangest species among social theorists are those individuals who want the state to be reduced to a minimum but not be abolished altogether. While it is not surprising that a socialist wants a state because he has no idea of economics, the minarchist already knows about the advantages of a free market economy.

He wants to reduce the state to a minimum for precisely the reason that the market is better suited to distributing resources efficiently. But why should economic laws not apply to such an important commodity as security? Even if the minarchist wants to limit the tasks of the state to the protection of property rights, how many resources does he want to make available for this? There are no market prices. Should half the population work for the police or only ten percent?

The minarchist also denies an iron law of human action: people seek their own advantage, so those who possess power want even more power. That's why every state expands. Even the US, which has the most libertarian constitution there has ever been, is now a violent and, with regard to foreign policy, aggressive police state.

Even a minarchist like Roland Baader admitted in various places that the supporters of a private law system had the better arguments. His attitude is, he said, more like a gut feeling. In my opinion, the rejection of anarchy has something to do with one of the strongest feelings of all: fear of the unknown.

It's only natural. The unknown and the foreigner always represent higher risks. Most people are only afraid because there is no PLS anywhere at the moment and nobody has experienced it live. Even the reference to numerous examples of historical private law systems, which I will describe in another book, does not satisfy most of them. They are not wrong to argue that nobody knows exactly whether they really worked as well as libertarian historians describe them.

But I can reassure these people. A private law system is nothing more than a free market. And markets exist all over the world. Black markets, for example, are everywhere, even in communist states. Even in the place easiest for the state to monitor, in prison, there is a drugs market. Of course, these markets are less efficient because the prohibition increases the risk and thus the price, while the quality is worse compared to a legal market. A drug buyer, for example, cannot sue his dealer for bad goods because he would have to go to the state. Therefore, contaminated drugs are more common, which is the main reason for most drug-related deaths. But ultimately the market does its job: it brings supply and demand together.

While markets are functioning everywhere in the world at all times, nowhere in the world has there ever been a state that would have worked and not collapsed at some time. The states that exist today are all relatively young and the signs of disintegration are obvious to everyone. Either they will first merge into a larger supranational structure or they will decay again into smaller individual parts, but they do not remain stable. The market always remains the market.

Democracy, the God that failed

You should by now have lost all illusions about democracy. But it's a hard thing to give up something you've believed in all your life. Therefore, I would like to provide you here with my disenchantment with the most important myths of democracy from my book "Die Vereinigten Staaten von Europa". For me the decisive parable is this:

Imagine you get on a bus and then start discussing with the other passengers about where the trip should be going. After endless debates, they vote on the destination. The majority decides. In the end, however, almost everyone would be unhappy, except the one who perhaps arrives exactly at the destination he was aiming for.

It would be better, of course, if everyone simply chose the bus that leads exactly to their destination. This is the private law system. The common bus is the state. State means endless debates and dissatisfied passengers. Anarchy does not mean debates, but conflict-free choices.

The state is institutionalized conflict. Anarchy is harmony. The state is chaos. Anarchy is order. Do you wonder why the state is telling you the exact opposite?

The analogy also appears briefly in the following passages from my book. I've removed the sources, but of course they're in the book:

If there is one thing about which (almost) all people in the West agree, it is that democracy is the best of all forms of society. Winston Churchill boiled this attitude down to an essence:

Democracy is the worst form of government except for all the other forms that have been tried from time to time.

That's pretty much what most people think. Many are at odds with the real existing politics, but think that there is no alternative to democracy. We have already seen that the private law society is an alternative, but few know it. Since the myth of democracy is so wide-spread, I will deal with it in more detail, also because the European Union is to be made increasingly palatable to us with the fact that we only have to make it more "democratic" and everything would be in the best of order. In fact, the EU is extremely undemocratically organised; even if it were "democratized", this would not solve any of the problems.

The Dutch authors Frank Karsten and Karel Beckman have put together the greatest myths of democracy in their excellent book "Wenn die Demokratie zusam-menbricht" (Engl.: "Beyond Democracy"); this is what I am leaning on in the following, but I recommend rea-ding the whole book.

The most important element in propaganda is constant repetition. Every day we hear songs of high praise about democracy, so that some effort is necessary to free ourselves from this propaganda.

Myth 1: Every vote counts

This myth is quickly refuted. You are one of 60 million voters in Germany. So you can calculate pretty exactly how much your vote counts: one sixty millionth. Imagine if you had a sixty millionth of an influence on what you wear tomorrow. You'd look like the Wolpertinger. The authors are therefore correct to write:

Voting means the illusion of influence in exchange for the loss of freedom.

Myth 2: In a democracy the people prevail

Karsten/Beckman quote a Dutch comedian who once put it in a nutshell:

Democracy is the will of the people. Every morning I read with surprise in the newspaper what I want.

Of course, there is no such thing as the will of the people. Someone wants this, someone else wants that. Another contradiction is the argument that the parties are necessary because people do not have the expertise to make complicated economic decisions. But how can they then understand the parties' election manifestos, which nobody reads anyway? Do politicians have a secret miracle cure that gives them inexhaustible wisdom? How is it then that the parties' concepts are different (different in the methodology of the robbery)?

The reality is that the parties are doing what the lobbyists closest to them want them to do. On the left these are the trade unions, which mainly fill their pockets through training companies and enjoy special rights, on the green side it's the suppliers of "renewable energies" and on the right perhaps a steel or car company which is helped with subsidies. The „libertarian" FDP in Germany protects pharmacists from competition or reduces taxes for hoteliers instead of for everyone.

All the parties together are feeding customers to the insurance industry via crackpot ideas such as the state subsidized Riester or Rürup pensions, who then buy worthless bonds from the state. All parties also adhere to the central bank, the state-owned cartel of major banks. Of course, none of that is for the benefit of the "people" at all. The best help for citizens would be if they were allowed to keep their own money to buy every service themselves.

Myth 3: The majority is right

This is probably one of the strangest and at the same time most widespread errors. First, majorities obviously fluctuate. Sometimes red rules, sometimes blue. How can the majority be right in both cases? Karsten/Beckman very aptly quote the British politician and writer Auberon Herbert on the logic and morality of democracy:

Five men are in a room. Because three men take one view and two another, have the three men any moral right to enforce their view on the other two men? What magical power comes over the three men that because they are one more in number than the two men, therefore they suddenly become possessors of the minds and bodies of these others? As long as they were two to two, so long we supposed each man remained master of his own mind and body; but from the moment that another man, acting Heaven only knows from what motives, has joined himself to one party or the other, that party has become straightaway possessed of the souls and bodies of the other party. Was there ever such a degrading and indefensible superstition? Is it not the true lineal descendent of the old superstitions about emperors and high priests and their authority over the souls and bodies of men?

Myth 4: Democracy is politically neutral

Since theoretically every party can be elected, the impression arises that every party, every ideology has the same chance. In fact, democracy itself is an ideology, the idea that we have to decide everything together. Democracy is therefore by definition a collectivist idea. Karsten/Beckman write:

There are basically no limits to collectivization. If the majority (or rather the government) wants it, they can decide that we all have to wear armour when we walk the streets because it is safer. Or we all have to dress up like clowns because it makes people laugh. No individual freedom is sacred.

Or the government can force people to wear useless face masks as seen in the coronavirus crisis, I might add. According to the British business magazine The Economist of 17 March 2011, government spending in the western democracies of Europe and the USA has, since 1870, risen from 10 to just under 50 percent of GDP - and has done so consistently. Even Sweden was still at 5.7 percent in 1870 and even the allegedly free USA now has 43 percent. And those are just the official figures.

In reality, the state now intervenes in almost every business, but this is not reflected in the public spending ratio. For example, bus routes along railway lines in Germany were banned for 80 years. This was relaxed at the beginning of 2013 – oh miracle — by the coalition, so that now long-distance bus transport between cities is allowed, with the result that prices are falling dramatically. SPD Chancellor candidate Peer Steinbrück came up with nothing better than to warn against too low (!) prices: "Dumping prices", especially in city tourism, could lead to the long-distance bus being chosen instead of the package tour.

Apart from such tiny exceptions, however, the trend towards more regulation remains unbroken. The EU is the master of this madness. A regulation on the length of a pacifier cord (sic!) comprises 52 pages (DIN EN 12586) and thus more words than the Basic Law. Just as I am writing this, there is news that the EU is planning to ban olive oil — a natural preservative, by the way — in open carafes on restaurant tables. Thank God! Millions of people have been saved from death by olive oil!

Thousands of such ludicrous laws with thousands of pages and hundreds of thousands of words are enacted each year anew. American federal laws now contain 3.8 million words. The Ten Commandments and the American Declaration of Independence managed with almost 300 words. And basically, three of the Ten Commandments (do not kill/injure, steal, lie/cheat) are enough. Every single law deprives people of the freedom to make voluntary agreements with each other. Karsten/Beckman therefore conclude:

In fact, democracy is essentially a totalitarian ideology, though not as extreme as Nazism, fascism or communism.

It does, however, lead straight to it, I might add.

Myth 5: Democracy leads to prosperity

Many people think we owe our prosperity to democracy. Politicians foment this thesis. The EU, too, is constantly attributed with having some share in the wealth generated by its citizens. The opposite is true. We owe German prosperity, for example, solely to the fortunate fact that Ludwig Erhard introduced a relatively free market economy in Germany. There are enough undemocratic states such as Singapore, Monaco or Liechtenstein that are considerably more successful than Germany. The only important factor is the extent to which individual rights, especially property rights, are protected.

The advantage for the weak of a market economy, with secure property rights and freedom of contract, can be proven not only logically but also empirically. For example, the Fraser Institute's annual Economic Freedom Report (note: the figures refer to an older report, but the relative figures have not changed much) shows that the average citizen earns 6.9 times more in the countries with the highest economic freedom than in the countries with the lowest economic freedom. But the poorest 10 percent earn 8.2 times as much as the poorest in the countries with the lowest freedom.

The richest are unfortunately not shown, but this is not relevant really (they will probably profit even less, because the average is already below the value for the poorest). What is important is that the poorest earn 8 times as much as the poorest in the most heavily regulated countries and even twice as much as the average citizen in the less free countries (8,735 dollars vs. 4,545 dollars).

In addition, in the countries with the highest economic freedom, life expectancy and the quality of education are higher, health care is better and the number of poor people is lower. As the individual analysis shows, the quality of health care and education is also higher where there is the least government intervention in precisely these areas. Although this cannot be summarised because the individual models are too different, it is clear that competition and the (voluntary) division of labor also produce better results in these areas. Especially since people would have three times as much money at their disposal to choose the best provider. What happens if the state takes care of these areas? To put it in a word from Ron Paul in his presidential debates: "Prices go up. Quality goes down. "

Every new law of the EU or the German government restricts individual freedom and thus ensures the destruction of prosperity and not its increase. Since, as has been shown, in democracies the state continues to expand, the opposite of what many people believe is true. Democracy does not create wealth, it destroys it. Democracy is not the solution to the problem, it is the problem.

Frank Karsten has described the mechanism very nicely in a guest article for the Party of Reason:

Democracy is like eating out with a hundred people who have previously decided to share the bill equally. If someone orders a delicious dessert for ten euros, he pays only ten cents and the others the rest. Because everyone feels the same incentive, the joint debt soon rises sharply, much higher than if everyone was paying for themselves.

In a democracy, all voters try to put their personal goals on the common bill. Pensioners vote for higher pensions, parents for "free" schoolbooks, farmers for even more agricultural subsidies, and so on. Everyone tries to win at the expense of the others, but everyone loses, like the guests in the example above. The politician who promises the most, no matter how unrealistic it is, usually wins the elections.

Myth 6: Democracy is necessary to ensure a fair distribution of wealth and to help the poor

As shown in the previous section, the less the state intervenes, the better off the poor are. Democracies are extremely vulnerable to lobbying. Lobbying companies are the main beneficiaries of redistribution. A study by a Dutch government (!) agency in 2011 concluded that higher income groups benefit most from state subsidies. For example, two fifths of the EU budget is spent on agricultural subsidies. Among the largest recipients of these subsidies are food companies and even energy suppliers such as RWE or the airline Lufthansa! RWE received it because the company purchased agricultural land for lignite mining, and Lufthansa received it for the sugar and milk it offered passengers.

If people have more disposable income, even charitable associations receive more funds. They know better than any bureaucrat who actually needs the help. If it becomes apparent that a charity is misusing funds, you can decide to donate to another charity overnight. In the meantime, there are even rating agencies that evaluate how much of the donated money for the respective organisation actually goes to the needy. It is highly unlikely that such funds will go to some corporation, and if they do, it will mean the end of that organization as soon as it becomes known. The state, on the other hand, always remains. Only the puppets of the corporations are exchanged.

Myth 7: Democracy is necessary for harmonious coexistence

As Hans-Hermann Hoppe has shown, the state regularly generates conflicts instead of avoiding them. Karsten/Beckman also offer two illustrative examples:

Suppose we were to decide democratically how much and what kind of bread is baked every day. This would lead to endless lobbying, campaigns, bickering, meetings and protests ... Democracy is like a bus full of people who have to decide together where the driver is going. The progressives vote for San Francisco, the conservatives prefer Dallas, the libertarians (and me; OJ) want to go to Las Vegas, the Greens (and me; OJ) want to go to Woodstock and the rest in a thousand other directions.

Anyone who has ever had a political discussion knows how quickly it can become emotional. Democracy is conflict. Market economy is cooperation. When everyone voluntarily chooses a service, no one has to argue with anyone. If the performance is poor, you will at most come into conflict with your provider, who you can simply change if in doubt. But you will never quarrel with other customers — apart from during the summer sales. It was probably forbidden by politics for this reason.

Myth 8: Democracy is indispensable for a sense of community

Look at Greece and Spain. Forced community is not a community, but a prison. As explained, democracy foments conflict rather than avoids it. Only voluntary togetherness generates a sense of community, as everyone can verify through his personal life. Some people may have experienced this when they were "forced" by the circumstances to sit in the opponent's fan block at a football match, or when their parents forced them to visit Aunt Else.

Myth 9: Democracy is the same as freedom and tolerance

Admittedly, freedom and tolerance are more pronounced in democracies than in malicious dictatorships. But they also exist and existed in monarchies. In a private company these values would be sacrosanct. In democracies freedom is increasingly being curtailed, and how much tolerance is diminishing can, I believe, be very well understood by everyone who regards today's reality. Aristotle wrote over 2,000 years ago: *Unlimited democracy, like the oligarchy, is a tyranny extended to a large group of people.* The smallest minority is the individual. And it has no freedom if it depends on a real or theoretical majority.

Myth 10: Democracy promotes peace and helps fight corruption

The democratic USA has begun by far the most wars in the past 100 years. In fact, they're the only state that's ever used nuclear weapons. Yet countless other countries that do not even possess these weapons are considered rogue states. This does not mean, of course, that everything is fine in these countries, quite the contrary. But obviously democracy is no guarantor of peace.

In the allegedly peaceful EU, the crisis created by the state and democratically decided monetary system has led to conditions that are in part similar to civil war — and the worst is yet to come. Even the death penalty has already been introduced through a back door in the Lisbon Treaty, but without the mass media, as part of the political-media complex, taking it up. So you can see that even in a democracy that is supposedly an open society, it is possible to simply hide such things. Without the Internet practically nobody would know about it at all.

One variant of the myth says that democracies do not wage war against each other, but that is not true either. Since NATO was founded, its members have not fought wars with each other. But that has little to do with the fact that they are democracies, but with the common alliance. On the contrary: Until the 18th century, monarchs hired mercenary troops, while many democracies introduced compulsory military service, which affected the civilian population much more. And that democratic politicians are not corrupt does not have to be commented on further. It's just not called corruption, it's whitewashed as lobbying.

Myth 11: There is no better alternative

You already know that the private law society provides an alternative. But I want to go back over what now, in the obvious crisis of democracy, is being offered to us as an alternative, namely "More democracy!" or "Real democracy now!". There are indeed initiatives with names like these. It will take you a long time to find a more intolerant bunch than these groups. If you appear there as a libertarian in a forum, you will be thrown out faster than you can say "freedom". They are often left-wing extremists who consider a libertarian to be on the right just because he is not on the left.

More democracy is an illusion. By definition, more democracy means more collectivism, less individual freedom. The ideas of these groups read accordingly. For example, the demand for an "unconditional basic income" (UBI). This means that one takes away money from people who work and gives it to others who do not work. The latter do not even have to give reasons or be in need. This is a result of decades of brainwashing by the state. People actually think they have a right to be unconditionally financed by others. A complete perversion of the idea of solidarity — apart from the fact that it is economically nonsensical.

The easiest way to end a discussion on this topic is to ask: Why didn't Götz Werner, founder of the dm drugstore chain and prominent UBI propagandist, just pay his employees 1000 euros a month and let them decide whether they want to come to work or not? The term itself is a prime example of Orwell's Newspeak: UBI is neither unconditional nor an income. An income is by definition something you get for a service. And the condition is that the money is taken away from someone else.

Something still worth discussing would be more direct democracy. This can often prevent the worst. For example, people would never have agreed to the Lisbon Treaty, the euro or mass immigration. However, Switzerland, for example, also shows the downsides of direct democracy. Thus, minarets were banned there by referendum, although it would of course be up to the owners to decide what they build on their property, as long as this was not accompanied by noise pollution from a muezzin calling out loudly for prayer. Also, there are to be referenda on minimum wages (of 22 Swiss francs = 22 euros!), which could soon become the basic income.

Switzerland's advantage lies less in direct democracy than in decentralization. The competition between the cantons means that people can vote with their feet and simply move away when things go too far for them. More rights for the municipalities, especially tax sovereignty, would also be a good solution for Germany or the United States. As soon as the state authorities or fellow citizens become too intrusive or exploitative via the ballot box, one could move to another city or community without having to leave the country, culture, language, family and friends completely. When the productive people can leave the community at any time, this can really focus minds.

Since it is rather unlikely that the states will abolish themselves overnight, systematic decentralization is therefore the most important political demand. Most people understand this without having to have any knowledge of economics. The slogan is simple: Where the problems arise, they should also be solved. Period.

There is a worldwide trend towards secession. Regions want to become independent again. First, because they have had enough of orders from the central government, and second, because of economic constraints. Ethnic reasons are usually only the emotional reason, in the end it is all about the wallet. An area that secedes is no longer liable for the debts of the central government or the neighbors. Munich (see my "Plan M") or Bavaria could get rid of their euro debts and their contribution to the fiscal equalization scheme overnight. If the economic crisis worsens, this will happen anyway. Each region can declare itself independent under international law. Theoretically, this can also be done by an individual, only in that case the state power won't be impressed.

The social question

But how can citizens provide for themselves without the state? I'll start with a text from "Die Vereinigten Staaten von Europa":

Most risks are privately insurable. And much cheaper than today. The so-called private health insurance funds are regulated from beginning to end. They are only allowed to pay what the pharmaceutical lobby permits them to do through the regulatory authorities. The statutory health insurance funds are cross-subsidized. Even under these bad circumstances, there are private health insurance companies where you can insure yourself for 100 euros a month, with a correspondingly high deductible of around 3,000 euros. But you can afford it if you earn much more net. All that matters is that you're covered for the difficult cases.

Insurance against total disability, for example, costs less than 10 euros a month. It wouldn't be the state that would permit drugs, the screening of which is financed by the pharmaceutical company itself, which means that the result is certain from the outset. Private health insurers would be able to say exactly which medication or natural remedy really helps and is the cheapest on the basis of their own tests and above all the evaluation of their patient data.

A healthy, long-living customer is in the interest of the insurance company because the costs are low and he pays premiums for as long as possible. Today, insurers must adhere to the guidelines of the state influenced by lobbyists.

The only risk that is difficult to insure is unemployment. At best, the trade unions could be trusted to establish a system that would be voluntarily accepted by the members. They are unlikely to force unemployed people into some one-euro job, but could offer them to work for the union. If the unemployed person refuses, the union knows very well that he is a notorious re-fusenik.

In fact, unions historically offered all kinds of insurance benefits, until the state — led by Bismarck in Germany — took the business out of their hands to win votes or protect lobby interests. In principle, however, risks over which one has too much influence cannot be insured. There is, however, an ancient and proven secret recipe against it: Save! The time to save money is when you have some! Without compulsory state levies you would have saved so much after three years that you could bridge ten years of unemployment. Then no one will tell you that you have to accept one-euro jobs. You have the time and peace to sort the offers, of which there are many more in a free market economy, anyway.

Important: If you save for your own old age, you are not bound to any terms. You could, for example, save in gold, the value of which is increasing anyway as a result of technological progress, corresponding to an increase in productivity of around 3 percent a year. From these savings you could then take the money for the deductible at the health insurance or the bridging of short-term frictional unemployment. Of course, you will miss that money in old age, but in a free market economy search unemployment is very short. It usually lasts a few weeks. This does not have a big effect on your total savings for old age. In my book „New World

Order exposed" I calculate that an unskilled cleaning woman with an hourly wage of 10 euros or dollars would be a millionaire in her old age.

There's still one case to settle: What about a young person who wants to start a career but can't find a job? He doesn't have any money to protect himself. Quite simple: As during the 18 years before, he lives with his parents and they continue to pay his insurance until he finds a job. The parents also know better than the anonymous "society" of taxpayers whether the offspring is a lazy-bones or simply unlucky when looking for a job. It is also the parents who insure the children against disability, chronic illness or inability to work. The risks are low at birth and cost only a few euros a month.

Numerous charitable institutions, such as the churches, take care of those who are in need despite all that. The state disciples do not believe this, but it is also part of the nature of humans that they are social, otherwise they would not easily fall for the supposedly "social" parties. Billions are donated every year; for the tsunami victims alone, Germans donated over 670 million euros. Of course, it would be much more if citizens had more money in their pockets.

Social responsibility is a natural accompaniment to a society based on the principle of non-violence and responsibility. History also proves this.

The greatest trick of the state is to expropriate its citizens through the monetary system. The second biggest trick is to make the companies accomplices and let them collect the taxes and levies. The psychological effect of this cannot be overestimated. On average, the German state now deducts 70 percent of its citizens' income, while it spends only three percent of the gross domestic product on the security of its citizens — on the justice system and defense.

However, the citizen don't realize it. Social security contributions and income tax are deducted directly from wages. Indirect taxes such as VAT and mineral oil tax are collected by traders. To free yourself from this psychological trap, simply do the following thought experiment: Take your current net monthly salary, multiply it by three and then by twelve. And now imagine you would have to pay two thirds of that sum at the end of the year in one fell swoop. With a net amount of 1.500 Euro per month that would be 36.000 Euro! I maintain that if citizens had to pay all taxes and duties in one fell swoop at the end of the year, we would have a revolution before tomorrow morning.

Poverty is essentially a welfare state phenomenon. The state creates its own demand. It used to be good manners for the wife to volunteer because her husband's salary was sufficient. Before the simultaneous introduction of the FED and income tax, there were probably more women volunteering than needy people in the US. Since this is not the main theme of my book, I refer you to the Austrian School. Many authors have devoted themselves to this topic. Free articles and books can be found mainly at the Ludwig von Mises Institute in Germany and America.

I will conclude with an example that you will certainly be able to understand yourself. If a friend of yours lost his job, hearth and home for any reason, would you take him in for a few weeks until he got back on his feet? I would think so. Usually you have several friends, and somebody is prepared to help. I've done this several times already.

Once I took in a friend who had been chucked out of his apartment and had no job at all. He assured me he was eager to find a job, but he couldn't find one. That seemed suspicious to me, because after all, we lived in Munich, a city with a very low unemployment rate. One day I grabbed him and walked with him across Leopoldstraße, where I lived. To the left and right I showed him notices where jobs were offered. He had a different excuse at every job why he didn't want to apply. Of course it wasn't jobs as an actor (his actual profession, but he was without a shoot at the time), TV presenter or multi-billionaire, but waiters, bartenders, salesmen, furniture movers and so on.

Then I said to him:

"Look, why should I work for you when you're too delicate to take these jobs? I have been a cleaner before this, worked in the warehouse or sorted letters. Why should I accept that I can't take girls home anymore because you're hanging around on my couch?"

The last bit I said above all because this was my main concern and at that time our common favorite past-time and he couldn't take home any girl either. And do you know what? A few days later he had found a source of income and moved out. He still owes me money today. Give him my regards.

The state lacks this kind of social control. It doesn't know the people who want transfers from it. For this reason, it draws up all kinds of rules, some of which are meaningful, but others are meaningless. The more precise the rules are, the more unworldly they are. The less accurate they are, the more arbitrariness prevails.

Taking a friend in for a while is no big deal. The host buys the food for him and he in turn helps with the housekeeping. In a PLS there would be enough jobs, so that a stay would always be only temporary. The first point of contact is of course the family as the most important social association. That is why the state systematically destroys the family.

But honestly, even if someone doesn't have a family anymore: Someone who has no friends at all who would take him in temporarily is obviously not a very nice person. Then why should strangers feed him? You should also bear in mind that in Germany, one of the most developed welfare states in the world, more than 300,000 people are homeless, and according to other estimates even more. Obviously, even a state cannot prevent this.

There will always be people who, for whatever reason, can't get on their feet. The question is, how do we deal with it? The state obviously can't. To care for these homeless people costs less than is already being donated today. The money today mostly flows abroad because the state creates the illusion that it already takes care of everyone.

The only solution

You should now not only have understood that a private law system would work. Above all, you should understand that the abolition of the state *is the only solution*. Every state degenerates at some point. Even if the wisest and kindest people were at the head of the state, it could not work. Even the wisest ruler cannot know how many resources to use on which problem. Ludwig von Mises and Nobel laureate Friedrich August von Hayek have already demonstrated why socialism cannot function: Because there are no market prices that show which goods are in short supply.

This also applies, of course, to the good "security". A state cannot distribute resources efficiently, i.e. it cannot really ensure security. In order to explain to you this rather technical expression of the efficient distribution of resources in a more specific way, I would like to give you an example that is particularly striking in developing countries, but which applies everywhere:

If a new building or residential complex is erected somewhere, shops immediately settle in the area: Supermarkets, hairdresser's, stationery stores and so on. For example, if the hairdresser is constantly fully booked, one of the employees might start their own or a new person might discover the situation for himself. There'll be more hairdressers. At some point someone goes broke because they don't get enough customers. There's only a limited number of them. That's what economists mean when they say prices show which goods are scarce.

The worst hairdresser, or the one who arrived too late, can no longer assert his prices, so he gives up. Customers are hardly aware of these processes. All they see is that there's always a hairdresser near them. This is how every market works. It also makes it clear how harmful a nationwide minimum wage is. In some areas in East Germany, hairdressers earn less than the current minimum wage. Without taxes, levies and inflation, they would have three times as much. But jobs simply disappear because those who can't afford it simply go to the hairdresser less often or cut their own hair.

If you're sitting opposite someone you want to convince of the value of a stateless society, just ask them where all the beautiful things they own come from: their shirt, their trousers, their watch, their cell phone, their sunglasses, their car. Mrs. Merkel or Mr. Trump has given no order to provide him with these things.

Pick out a product that is manufactured by a particularly large corporation, such as the mobile phone manufacturer. It's certainly a billion-dollar corporation. Ask your friend if the company forced him to buy the device. If he says no, ask him why not? When, according to the prevailing left ideology, this billion-dollar corporation would have to be so terribly powerful that it could do anything? It simply can't. Only the state can force him to buy certain goods, such as overpriced windmill electricity.

Now all your counterpart needs to do is transfer this knowledge to the market for security. At least you might have made a contemporary who is interested in social issues sufficiently curious to investigate the evil issue of anarchy. He is ripe for this or other books on a private law system.

Perhaps your counterpart wants to achieve one of the following goals:

More security, better environmental protection, greater prosperity, less poverty, no more wars, more natural remedies, higher penalties for malicious corporations, better protection of children, more effective protection of animals, breaking the power of the establishment, making the deep state disappear, no taxes, no coercive fees, less propaganda, fewer lies, less terror, no un-controlled mass immigration, a peaceful culture or simply to be left alone.

Tell him there's only one solution: A natural order, from people for people who voluntarily agree on something. Hooligans don't stand a chance.

Technologies of the future

There are many historical examples of functioning private law systems, but one thing is clear: today a PLS would work much better thanks to technology. Mobile phones could, for example, provide an app where you can film and report a crime at the touch of a button. The app could automatically send out an alarm if you are in danger. Such applications already exist today.

The same applies if you think you have discovered a wanted criminal. You could photograph him and upload the picture to the app for download by the security service provider. You should not upload such a picture on public networks, because you are also liable if you get an innocent person into trouble. Therefore, your insurance company would require you to make the data available only to professionals.

Every technology can be used for good as well as for evil. You should by now have realised how the competition for voluntarily paying customers leads to technology being used primarily for good. Information technology would also mean that many more people would learn much more quickly about good solutions. If, for example, there were still states, but a small area would already be transformed into a functioning private legal order, this information would also go around the world without mass media.

Only the truth counts

Have I promised you too much? I didn't torment you with moral and philosophical questions. You can comprehend everything with your own common sense, without having studied economics. We live in a time of relativism, but there are ultimate truths. There are three types of statements, those that are true, those that are false, and empirical statements. False and empirical statements are worthless. For example, the statement that 35 percent of people prefer wooden chairs. The compilation of this data may be incorrect. Opinions can change. This is contrary to statements that are true in themselves, such as: A good that I consume today I can no longer consume tomorrow. A cake that I eat today, I can't eat tomorrow.

My theses are based on such a true statement: The judge must not be a party to the conflict. That statement is simply true. Everything else follows from that. I was able to trace all the questions back to this basic statement, which suggests that we have really found the root of evil.

To give you an image of what awaits you: As a crime fan, you can imagine a private law system like this: The investigating detective is as brilliant as Columbo, Monk or the Mentalist. The lab's as good as CSI. The psychological skills of the investigators are as good as those of the Behavioral Analysis Unit (BAU) of Criminal Minds. This is otherwise only available on television, but it is precisely these skills that prevail in competing agencies. State police, on the other hand, can be compared to the cinema series "Police Academy".

Or this: A private legal system would be as good as American crime series are compared to German ones. In the latter case, the perpetrator usually simply confesses. Hardly ever is a case solved by outstanding skills in logical thinking in a well thought-out plot. State television produces crime thrillers that are about as good as state security. The series "Tatort" even managed to produce a thriller, in the middle of the biggest wave of crimes induced by foreigners ever seen in Germany, in which a good-hearted refugee became the victim of an evil neo-Nazi. That was too much propaganda even for the left-wing newspaper Süddeutsche Zeitung.

In order not to fall out with my Munich film friends, I would like to add that the ideological character also has to do with state film funding. Basically, the quality, especially in cinema, has improved a lot in recent years, probably because more and more film people are working and training in America. Creative writing is actually a profession that can be studied there. It's hard to believe.

In America, by the way, there was a TV series about a billionaire who with his technology company took over the police work in a district in Chicago. There the billionaire had an app distributed that could be used to report crimes. Probably due to political correctness, the entrepreneur in the series allowed himself to be dissuaded from offering his services to all people by a pretty, bleeding-heart policewoman, because then only "the rich" would profit. In Hollywood, even the Social Justice Warriors are pretty.

The series with the (very badly chosen) name APB was dropped after one season, although in my opinion it was just as well done as most successful American TV series. This may be because it immediately became clear to every viewer that it would be better to have the police work done by competing companies. The basic plot of the series is that the mayor has promised that the billionaire could also take over other police districts if he succeeds. The viewer thus immediately recognises that a private provider has an incentive to work well.

By the way, the series was inspired by an article in the New York Times on July 30, 2015. It's about a wealthy businessman who implemented a similar concept in the French Quarter of New Orleans. Sydney Torres provided citizens with an app in which crimes can be reported, and sponsored a private police force.

The article begins with an example where the private intervention force was on the scene within two minutes, compared to an average of 28 minutes needed by the police. The resident who used the app explains to the reporter why: "Everyone in New Orleans knows that 911 is a lost cause." I add this remark: The private security guards earn more than the state police. The security people get rewards for successful missions, which is exactly the concept I describe in this book. I only discovered the article at the end of the book, but it's only logical that private companies would do the same.

The crime rates in the French Quarter fell dramatically of course and soon residents of the other areas complained that the criminals are now doing their mischief in their neighborhoods. This is exactly the civilizing process I've been writing about. If the other districts were to adopt the model, crime rates would of course fall there as well.

In fact, the entrepreneur now has numerous inquiries from all over the country. By the way, he got rich with a garbage removal company. Since the state garbage collection in New Orleans was also a disaster, he had started to transport the garbage himself. One day he put his name on the trucks. After that he was inundated with orders and became rich. That's how it works, the evil, evil market. And for people who aren't so quick to think: According to state schools, garbage collection is also a public task that only the benevolent and all-knowing state can accomplish.

New Orleans is not an isolated case. More and more private companies are taking on police work. According to the NY Times article, there are already three times more private security forces in the USA than state ones. But even in European countries like Norway or Estonia there are already more private security guards than state policemen. The example of Oakland shows that I was absolutely right with my estimates of what private security costs. When crime rates there rose by 50 percent within three years, some citizens were fed up in 2013. They launched a crowdfunding campaign, which was funded within two days, and commissioned a private company to run patrols. The cost: 50 US cents per day and citizen.

Private companies have long provided security in gated communities. The main reason for their emergence was the dissatisfaction of the citizens with the public services. By the way, the concept became really popular in the USA in the 1980s. In Starret City, a gigantic building complex with 20,000 inhabitants, 5,500 apartments and 57 buildings, the inhabitants were guarded by private security. The complex is located in the middle of what was then the worst part of Brooklyn, at that time already the stronghold of crime in New York. A 1986 study found that although residents reported crimes more frequently than the population average, there were only 6.57 crimes per thousand residents, instead of 49.86 in the district where the building complex was located.

Not surprisingly, such concepts make their first foothold where the crime rate is highest and therefore the need is greatest. In Honduras in 2017, the president campaigned to create zones where private companies would take over everything from police, law enforcement and prisons to the judiciary. We may soon see him on the board of directors of such a company. Honduras may host the first private city in the world. Check out the book "Free Private Cities" by Titus Gebel to learn more about the concept.

And if you're still skeptical that some mafia company will take over at some point: Only two percent of Germans commit crimes every year. Everyone else has an interest in them, and not innocent people, being prosecuted. That means 98 percent of people vote with their wallets every day to see who's best at keeping them safe, and you don't even have to debate it with the others.

Companies have long let their conflicts be decided by private court companies. Why wouldn't the common man be allowed to do that? In the Philippines I once met an Australian in a beach bar who lived on a boat. He was the silent type, so I had to talk. I explained to him the concept of the neutral judge from the second chapter and said the state must therefore be abolished. He looked at me and said, "You're right." I was afraid he just didn't feel like having a debate and asked:

"Do you really believe me? What do you do for a living?"

His answer: "I negotiate contracts for companies."

The next beer was on me.

If you still have a hint of an illusion that the state means well with you, I have, in conclusion, a fascinating numerical comparison for you. In Denmark, a study by the University of Copenhagen found that 75 per cent of the supposedly underage "refugees" examined were in fact adults.

At least 43 percent of the allegedly underage "refugees" in Germany are also adults, according to a source from the Family Ministry. But there are probably even more, because the "FAZ" writes:

It has been estimated by carers that even among migrants classified as minors, many are likely to be of legal age.

On average (!) German authorities pay out 5,250 euros per month per refugee classified as a minor, according to information from the Ministry of Family Affairs, according to "Zeit" dated 22 February 2017. It should be noted that a large part of the money is spent on people who have already entered illegally — via a safe third country —, who have never paid a cent into the system and who have also cheated on their details, i.e. who are criminals. We remember that the state spends 50 euros per month per citizen on their security (80 euros including the military). In other words, the state spends one hundred times as much money on foreign criminals as it spends on the security of a righteous local citizen who pays his taxes dutifully. Or just look at the draconian measures that the state has imposed in the wake of the coronavirus crisis, including compulsory vaccinations in some countries, even though real journalists like myself have pointed out from the start that the virus is at worst just a harmless flu. Still having illusions?

So let's remember:

The state exploits. Companies create wealth. Democracy is conflict. Anarchy is harmony. The state is chaos. Anarchy is order. That's the truth of the matter. Now you know why the state tells you exactly the opposite. Lying is inherent to its nature, as Nietzsche realized when he let Zarathustra speak:

A state, is called the coldest of all cold monsters.
Coldly lieth it also; and this lie creepeth from its mouth:
"I, the state, am the people."
It is a lie! Creators were they who created peoples, and hung a faith and a love over them: thus they served life. Destroyers, are they who lay snares for many, and call it the state: they hang a sword and a hundred cravings over them.

Where there is still a people, there the state is not understood, but hated as the evil eye, and as sin against laws and customs.

This sign I give unto you: every people speaketh its language of good and evil: this its neighbour understandeth not. Its language hath it devised for itself in laws and customs.

But the state lieth in all languages of good and evil; and whatever it saith it lieth; and whatever it hath it hath stolen.

Made in the USA
Coppell, TX
04 December 2022

87759928R00125